The Essentials of Competent Communication

AN INTERPERSONAL ANALYSIS

Revised First Edition

Jayi Thompson, M.A.

Anderson Jerrold Publishing Company
CHATSWORTH, CALIFORNIA

Anderson Jerrold Publishing Company
P.O. Box 3162, Chatsworth, CA 91313   www.ajpcompany.com

Ordering Information:
Quantity sales. Special discounts are available on quantity purchases by corporations, associations, and others. For details, contact the "Special Sales Department" at the address above.

The Essentials of Competent Communication/Jayi Thompson. — Revised 1st ed. ISBN 978-0-692-84192-1

The Essentials of Competent Communication

AN INTERPERSONAL ANALYSIS

Table of Contents

Preface

BACKGROUND AND PHILOSOPHY

The past nineteen years of consultative sales experience, teaching interpersonal communication skills, reviewing countless interpersonal text- books and journal articles revealed a particular need: a textbook (and course) focused on applied interpersonal communication. Essentially, one that allows students to learn and practice the specific skills required to get their goals met in a manner that enhances (or at least maintains) their relationships.

There seems to be countless textbooks on the topic of interpersonal communication that go into great detail about important theoretical issues and concepts. Pages and pages discussing topics like: should interpersonal communication be defined as quantitative or qualitative, the differences between our public and private selves, and how to use a "Johari Window" to understand your level of self-disclosure in a particular situation. I've studied many of these texts, and they provide a great depth of research and extremely detailed analysis of the concepts.

Although this textbook (and the course accompanying it) examines many of the same concepts, it has one particular goal in mind: increasing your communication competence through interactive participation. It aims to provide you with just enough details of the theoretical intricacies of interpersonal communication combined with practical applications of the concepts to empower you to get your goals met while enhancing (or at least maintaining) your relationships. That is the essence of communication competence.

The method used in the book (as well as the course) arose from my corporate professional experience working in Sales in media companies and educational experiences teaching today's diverse Community College student population. It focuses on a student's **D**esire to improve, **O**penness to self-analysis, **W**illingness to experiment, and **D**iscipline to study and inject what they learn into their behavior. Although the "DOWD" Method was created using the discipline of Communication, it's transferable to any discipline or field of study. Designed for this generation of student who is accustomed to fast-moving video clips, text messaging, and 140 character communication, the DOWD method requires:

1)   Accessible Reading- Making it rather short and straight to the point as possible.

2)   Providing Entertaining/Compelling Examples- Including excerpts from iconic films, well-known television sitcoms, self-reflective case studies, writing exercises, etc.

3)   Self-Analysis- Requiring self-reflection stimulated by Readings and Examples allowing students to identify themselves within the concepts.

4)   Behavioral Implementation- Students are challenged each week to apply what they learned into daily interactions.

Each lesson requires you to: 1) Read the textbook chapter, 2) Answer the questions that accompany the textbook reading and memorize those answers, 3) Complete the chapter's exercise (may be a film screening, case study, writing exercise, for hybrid courses "Start Here" book etc.) and answer the questions that accompany it, 4) Participate in class (face to face courses= classroom discussions, hybrid courses= discussion forum posts).

Finally, the ultimate goal of this book is to have every chapter, page, and word tell you a compelling story… a story about you… and just how dynamic you are. If you engage it, you will likely reap the benefits students have affirmed over and over again. They've said it motivated and empowered them to create better relationships with everyone they encounter.

Engage and enjoy the self-exploration!

Prof. J. Thompson

1

How We Work

What You Should Know

The 4 tools of Communication

Physical necessities

Identity necessities

Social necessities

Instrumental goals

Explain the Models of Communication

5 Principles of Communication

What You Should Do

Activities

- Watch the time codes from the film *Cast Away* and answer the questions that accompany it. You do not turn in the answers from *Cast Away* unless otherwise instructed.

Hybrid

- Post to the Cast Away discussion forum. Your 1st post (your answer to the discussion forum question) should be by Wednesday, but no later than Friday to earn points for the week. Remember to comment on other postings from at least 2 classmates by 5 p.m. on Sunday.

Reflection of the Week

How will understanding the models and the principles of communication help make you a better communicator?

Introduction

Can you recall the first time you took an Interpersonal Communication course? Was it in first grade, middle school, or maybe high school? Most often, college is the first time anyone takes an Interpersonal Communications course. Why is that? Of the four tools of communication, early education seems to focus on Reading, Writing, and Speaking, while the process of Listening is largely ignored. Elementary education primarily focuses on other disciplines like English, math, or science. Communication is not typically an independent field of study. One conclusion can be drawn from its absence in primary education: it is not thought to be as important as the other subjects. Perhaps it's because communication is so pervasive; it is assumed that everyone will learn enough about it simply by studying the other subjects. Whatever the reason, the goal of this chapter is to convey exactly how important communication is and to explain some basics regarding how it works.

Our Necessities

Learning how to communicate effectively is vital to our health and our very existence. There are many definitions for interpersonal communication, but for our purposes, we shall define it as an exchange of verbal and/or nonverbal messages between two individuals. According to Steven McCornack's book, *Reflect & Relate*, it is through these types of communication that we acquire our physical, identity and social necessities, and meet our instrumental goals.[1] First, let's address our physical necessities.

Physical Necessities

Studies have shown that:

• Socially isolated people are four times more susceptible to the common cold than those who have active social networks.[2]
• Divorced women and men's rate of all types of cancer is as much as five times higher compared to their married counterparts.[3]
• The likelihood of death increases when a close relative dies.[4]
• A lack of social relationships jeopardizes coronary health to a degree comparable to cigarette smoking, obesity, high blood pressure, and the lack of physical activity.[5]
• Divorced men (before age 70) die from heart disease, cancer, and strokes at double the rate of married men.[6]

Our entire lives, we have been told that our health can be positively maintained if we eat right, get the right amount of sleep, and exercise often. What does this research suggest about our physical versus our metaphysical selves? When speaking of our physical selves, we are referring to our bodies (the brain), while our metaphysical selves represent things beyond the physical like (our minds) love, our thoughts, and our emotions. The studies represent quite a contrast to what we have been traditionally taught about our health.

Identity Necessities

Regarding our identity needs, you have to ask yourself, do I consider myself tall? Am I smart, attractive, or perhaps clumsy? How do you come to such estimations about yourself without comparing yourself to others around you, often referred to as our reference group? All of these assessments, particularly when in our youth, are made by making social comparisons with others around us. Is your hair long or short? Do you have large or small hands? Think about how your answers can differ, depending on the reference group you are making the social comparison with.

Social Necessities

Have you ever felt the need to vent? Have you simply looked in the mirror and began speaking? Or have you reached out to someone to express yourself? It's likely that at one point or another, most if not all of us have or will. There have been a number of social needs identified that are satisfied through communication, including companionship, control, pleasure, relaxation, and affection.

Instrumental Goals

When visiting a hair salon or the barber, what instructions do you give the person styling your hair? Is it enough for you to just say, "Cut it" or "Take some off the top"? More than likely, you provide specific instructions for how you would like your hair to look, especially the first time you're allowing that person to style it. Having others act as we would like allows us to get our instrumental goals met.

□

Cast Away
Film Excerpts

- Consider what life would be like on a deserted island. How would you be able to survive if your needs weren't being met?

- You will be applying the information you just learned about our necessities when you watch the excerpts from *Cast Away*.

Communication Theories

The Sender sends a message using a channel (voice, radio, etc.), the message travels through noise, and the message reaches the Receiver who attempts to make sense of the message.

LINEAR versus TRANSACTIONAL

Now that we've established the importance of Interpersonal Communication as a worthy field of study to analyze something it helps to write it down. Take mathematics for example, we can verbally express "Two plus two equals four." However, that verbal expression can also be written as 2 + 2 = 4. It is vital to any field of study that it not only be expressed verbally but also nonverbally or in print. Since the early 21st century, theorists have attempted to capture what Interpersonal Communication looks like on paper. To this effort, two major theories have emerged: the Linear Model and the Transactional Model.[7]

Diagram 0.1

LINEAR MODEL

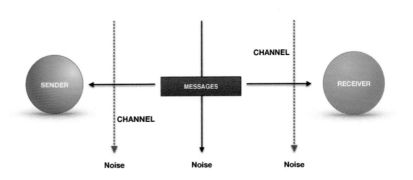

The Linear model of Communication is the elder of the two, originally conceived more as an analysis of radio communication than interpersonal interaction. It features a Sender and a Receiver. The Sender relays a message using a channel (for instance, a voice or radio), the message travels through noise, and the message reaches the Receiver who attempts to make sense of the message.

This simplistic model left many questions to be answered:

- When one person is communicating (sending a message), is the other person communicating at the same time?

- Although there always seems to be outside noise happening around us (external noise), are there internal noises that affect our reception and understanding of messages?

- Does everyone understand the meaning of a message the same way or differently?

Answering these questions is what leads us to analysis of the Transactional model of communication.

Diagram 0.2

TRANSACTIONAL MODEL

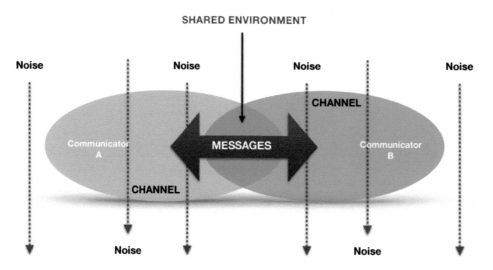

In many ways, the Transactional model is similar to the Linear. Specifically, there is a message being sent through a channel through noise, but the differences between the two models represent our focus.

First, rather than there being a Sender and Receiver, the Transactional model represents them as Communicator A and Communicator B. This change suggests that communication occurs simultaneously; we are sending and receiving messages (verbally and nonverbally) at the same time the other communicator is sending and receiving messages.

Second, the Linear and Transactional models recognize the existence of external noise, which can be anything from the sound of a television in the background to the tapping of pencils in the classroom. What the Transactional model includes, which is not in the Linear model, is internal noise. Do you know anyone that people say things like, "Don't talk to her before she has had something to eat" or "before he has had some rest"? Hunger and/or fatigue represent a few of the many conditions considered "internal noise", which affects our daily communication.

Third, the Transactional model recognizes that each individual has their own environment--past experiences that have helped form who that person is, how that individual thinks, and how they process information. However, there is an area in which our individual life experiences intersect; those are the area(s) of shared experience. It is sometimes referred to as the shared environment. Human beings, regardless of what language they speak, have a shared environment with every other human being on Earth due to shared experiences. Everyone has felt hunger, or fatigue, or illness. However, our shared experiences with other communicators tend to be much larger than that. People can both have an appreciation of art, football, Mexican food, movies, and many other things. When we identify our shared environment(s) with the other communicator, it makes it much more likely that we will get our instrumental goal met.

Think about a situation you encountered in the past with a stranger. Simply by communicating and learning the shared environment that existed between the two of you, you were able to get an instrumental goal met. The shared environment can be just about anything, from you and the other communicator being parents to both of you enjoying tennis. The key is to realize that you have shared experiences with everyone else on Earth. It is only a question of how many you have identified with the other communicator, making it more likely you'll meet your goal.

Creating a model that represents what Interpersonal communication looks like on paper is not an easy task. Communication is not just the words that we speak, but it's also nonverbal behaviors. Nonverbal communication can be much more subtle, occur in a micro-second, and be very ambiguous. We'll learn much more about this in future chapters. Currently, the Transactional model is the best representation of what Interpersonal communication looks like when it's written. But that doesn't mean that some current (or future) theorist won't come up with another model that better represents it.[8] Perhaps, it just might be you.

Principles of Communication

Once one grasps an understanding of the Models of Communication, it is important to focus on its principles. In her book, Interpersonal Communication: Competence & Concepts, Lane describes multiple principles of communication.[9] For our purposes, we'll focus on:

▫ **Principle 1** Communication can be Intentional or Unintentional There's an old, wise saying that people should pay less attention to what others say and more attention to what others do. When we communicate verbally, by definition it is intentional. No matter how quickly we speak, we have to process the words before they are spoken, making it intentional. Most often, our unintentional communication occurs nonverbally. For instance, we blush, cry, and/or sweat.

▫ **Principle 2** Irreversible How many times have you been in a fight or argument and said something, and the moment after it came out of your mouth you wanted to take it back? Those words said to our sibling, mate, or loved one never seem to go away. The other communicator repeats them often, and you just wish you never said it. Unfortunately, the best you can do is attempt to make up for the verbal damage caused by your poor choice of words.

□ Principle 3		All Behavior Communicates Something Every single action, as well as our choices to not act, can be interpreted by others. Meanings behind them can be attached to the action, whether intentional or unintentional. In other words, all behavior has communicative value. If you've

spent time around young children, you may have experienced them becoming angry and deciding they would "Not" communicate any more. They do this by going to the back of the room and sitting down facing the wall. They have decided to punish you by not communicating with you, but their behavior is communicating everything you need to know: they are upset, or frustrated, or unhappy. All behavior can be interpreted in one way or another. The problem is the potential inaccuracy of the interpretation. In Chapter 6 on nonverbal communication, we'll learn how we are constantly communicating nonverbal messages and how ambiguous nonverbal communication can be.

□ Principle 4		The Meaning of a Message Resides in the other Communicator Can you recall an experience when you said something you thought innocuous to someone, and it really made them upset? You certainly believed that what you said was no big deal, and you didn't have a negative intent, yet it

upset the other communicator. This often occurs because we have relationships with words that were formed our entire lives. When others use those words, more attention tends to be paid to the connotative meaning of the words than the denotative meaning. To communicate effectively, it helps to have a good understanding of the other communicator's emotive hot buttons and express ourselves as clearly as possible. The objective is to paint the picture in your head just as clearly to the other communicator.

□ Principle 5		Everything We Say Contains a Content and Relational Dimension Everything we say consists of the actual words AND the tone, speed, volume, pitch, etc. of how the words are said. If someone walks into the room and you say to her "Sit down", the content is clear, "Sit down." However,

how we feel about the other communicator greatly influences how we say the words. That's considered nonverbal communication; how we say something. If the other communicator is a child that you plan to discipline, you may sternly, in a loud voice say, "SIT DOWN" thus making the words a demand. But, what if it's your boss whom you have much respect for and whom your income depends on? You may use the exact same words (content), but the relationship with the other communicator changes how it's said, giving the content a different meaning. In a much softer, kinder voice, you ask "Sit down?" Those same words have now become a question or request rather than a demand. Based on how it was said, the entire meaning has changed. The relational dimension can determine the actual meaning of the content dimension.

Have you ever been in a situation in which you said (or someone said to you), "It's not what you said, but it's how you said it"? That statement is referring to the relational dimension, specifically it is the type of nonverbal communication called paralanguage (how something is said; tone, pitch, loudness, etc.). Our paralanguage can greatly influence our success in achieving an instrumental goal.

Key Reflections

To fully complete a topic/chapter, you must complete 4 steps: 1) Read the textbook chapter, 2) Answer the significant questions that accompany the textbook reading, 3) Complete the chapter exercise (may be a film screening, case study, writing exercise, etc.) and answer the questions that accompany it, 4) Participate in class (for face to face courses- classroom discussions, for hybrid courses- discussion forum posts).

After reading this chapter, answering the study guide questions, viewing the *Cast Away* excerpts and answering those significant questions; think about how important communication is in your life. How will understanding the models and the principles of communication help you become a better communicator and help you get your instrumental goals met more often?

These are some preliminary questions you should ask yourself when learning how to become a better communicator. In reality, achieving our goals is not enough. To really be successful, we all need to learn how to be more competent communicators across a multitude of interactions. This is our focus in Chapter 2 and in the rest of the text.

Chapter Activity 1

Significant Questions: Cast Away (2000)

Time Codes
1:06:45 – 1:15:17
1:26:35 – 1:31:30
1:40:33 – 1:45:18
Total= 19 minutes

1. How do we know that Chuck's physical needs are being met by Wilson's existence?

2. How do we know that Chuck's identity needs are being met by Wilson's existence?

3. How do we know that Chuck's social needs are being met by Wilson's existence?

4. Why do Chuck and Wilson have a fight?

5. What happens when Chuck finally loses Wilson for good, and he feels totally alone?

2

Competent
Communication

What You Should Know

The Definition of Communication Competence

Aspects of Communication Competence

Characteristics of Competent Communicators

What You Should Do

Activities

- Read and complete your answers to the "A" Student Brian Smith Accountability Case Study. You do not turn in the answers unless otherwise instructed.

Hybrid

- Post to the "Communication Competence" discussion forum. Your 1st post (your answer to the discussion forum question) should be by Wednesday, but no later than Friday to earn points for the week. Remember to comment on other postings from at least 2 classmates by 5 p.m. on Sunday.

Reflection of the Week

Write about a personal/professional interaction in which you believe you were a competent communicator (according to the definition in the textbook) and why?

Introduction

In our daily lives, we spend a large amount of time trying to get our instrumental goals met, meaning getting others to behave in ways we want them to. If getting our instrumental goals met was our only concern, perhaps we would all be thought of as manipulative, selfish beings. People do not like to feel used or disregarded. Competent communication requires us to preserve or strengthen the relationship, while getting our instrumental goals met is the next step in bettering our communication. Competent communicators avoid making others feel taken advantage of after they've achieved their goal.

However, competent communication cannot be achieved in every interaction or by any particular individual every time. Think of it more like an escalator, there are times when you elevate to the top and others when you are at the bottom. One goal of this book is to keep you moving upward across multiple communication interactions. As noted by Adler and Proctor, there are characteristics that influence our ability to achieve that goal.[1]

---

3 Characteristics of Competent Communication

□ *Characteristic 1: Competent Communication is Situational* Specific communication that is (or was) competent in one situation may not be in another. Simply stated; there is no ideal way to communicate across different situations. There are times when it is necessary to be more reserved in order to communicate competently and others in which competence can be reached by being sociable. Think about times when you have heard a joke that you thought was very inappropriate. More than likely, you were thinking that the joke was inappropriate for that particular situation. It is quite possible that you could think of situations that the joke would have been appropriate and considered funny to the audience.

□ *Characteristic 2: Competent Communication is Relational* Our relationship with the other communicator affects our ability to create competent communication. Think about times when you may have been competent communicating with a brother or sister, and you attempted the same communication with a friend, but you did not achieve the same result. The relationship with the other individual is vital when considering communication competence.

□ *Characteristic 3: Competent Communication is a Learned Skill* No one is born a competent communicator. Although our personality traits are passed down genetically, the people around us also have a great influence on how we communicate. Communication is a learned skill that is developed over time and greatly influenced by what we learn as children, for example, watching our parents, brothers, sisters, friends, and teachers communicate. We collected good and bad communication habits as children from the people around us, proving it very possible for us to learn positive habits that will lead us to more competent communication in the future.

Note

- The 3 Characteristics of Competent Communication can be thought of as general rules.

- While the 5 Characteristics of Competent **Communicators** can be thought of as learned behaviors.

---

5 Characteristics of Competent Communicators

Now that we have identified the 3 characteristics of competent communication, we're going to analyze the 5 characteristics of competent communicators. First, let's take a look at the difference between the two. When referring to competent communication, there are some fundamental attributes to consider. These are individual skills one acquires to be successful. Use the characteristics listed below as a checklist, not only to prepare for communication interactions but also to review interactions and measure their success.

◻
Characteristic 1: A Wide Range of Skills (Behaviors)   Competent communicators have a wide range of behaviors to choose from and demonstrate skills when performing those behaviors. In Chapter 3, all of the personality traits that are inside of us, from being talkative to being quiet or being ambitious to aimless, will be examined. It is the skill at performing these behaviors that can determine our competence in any particular situation. For example, if a peer is continuously talking to you in class, there are multiple ways to respond: You may simply be quiet and ignore the student until they stop talking, you may talk back to him or her, or ask your peer to stop talking.

Assuming that your instrumental goal is to get your classmate to stop talking, the range of behaviors and your skill level at performing the behavior go hand in hand in achieving your goal. However, if you are going to achieve it competently-- in a way that maintains or enhances the relationship--you will need to choose wisely.

◻
Characteristic 2: Ability to Choose the Correct Behavior at the Right Time (Self-Monitor)   It is great to have a wide range of behaviors to choose from and the skill to perform them, but if you can't choose the correct behavior at the right time, competence will be difficult to achieve. Is it the right time to attempt to be funny or imaginative or better to be quiet and self-controlled?

A key element to consider here is one's ability to self-monitor or your ability to understand your behavior from a detached perspective. In other words, look at your behavior and ask yourself, "Am I talking too much," or "Am I being too quiet?" If a person doesn't have the ability to self-monitor, it will be much more difficult to choose the appropriate behavior.

Along with self-monitoring, an important factor in choosing the correct behavior is your knowledge of the other communicator. If you know the other person well, and that that individual responds to humor or sarcasm, then you can feel more confident using those. If you don't know the other person well, you may be better advised to be careful or reserved.

□

Characteristic 3: *Ability to use Cognitive Complexity*

Cognitive complexity is the ability to view an issue from many different perspectives, allowing for multiple possibilities. Competent communicators are less likely to assume they know the reason why someone did something. For example, if your classmates didn't listen to something you said to them, you may assume that they were being rude. If you used cognitive complexity, you might think they didn't hear you, or they had to work the overnight shift at work, or they were paying attention to the instructor while you were talking. It is much more difficult to get instrumental goals met when we assume we know why other communicators say what they said or did what they did.

If you were to tell someone they were being rude, they may become defensive. They could be offended, thinking you made an incorrect assumption, rather than asking what their motivation was for the behavior. People can become defensive when others say things about them that they believe are untrue. It can get worse when someone assumes to know another communicator's motivation, i.e. why they behaved the way they behaved, without asking. Using cognitive complexity, goals can be accomplished competently much more often.

□

Characteristic 4: *Ability to use Sympathy or Empathy*

Sympathy is attempting to understand someone else's feelings from your perspective. Empathy is attempting to feel someone else's emotion or to place yourself in the other person's shoes. Competent communicators use both in the appropriate situations. By definition, sympathy is less emotional, thus takes less energy. Conversely, empathy uses more energy and is more emotional. In an Interpersonal communication interaction, one's ability to either understand someone's feelings or attempt to put oneself in someone's shoes is vital to being more competent. One thing to consider is which interactions are better suited for sympathy and which are better suited for empathy.

□

Characteristic 5: *Ability to be Self-effacing*

Finally, competent communicators don't take themselves too seriously. They have the ability to laugh at themselves and at mistakes they may make. We call this being self-effacing. Less competent communicators tend to have fragile egos, so they go to great lengths to protect them, acting as if every mistake is a strike against their very being, and as a result it can be more difficult for them to communicate competently. Competent communicators make mistakes and can laugh with others about them and still be secure in their intelligence, character, etc.

Key Reflections

After reading this chapter, answering the study guide questions, and completing the Brian Smith Accountability Case Study exercise, you should have viewed it as a model to increase your own competence. As foreshadowed in Chapter 1, you should have realized why simply getting one's instrumental goals met is not enough. In reflecting on your own interactions, this case study should have revealed areas you could practice to increase your level of communication competence.

Competent communicators have developed a certain level of confidence and a keen awareness of their personality traits, which allows them to properly use all 5 characteristics of competent communicators. The first step in increasing your own competence is to ask the question, "Who am I"? Answering this question is the focus of Chapter 3.

Chapter Activity 2

The Brian Smith Accountability
Communication Competence Case Study

The Paper Assignment

Professor Jessup announced that the final paper in her Philosophy 401 class had to be in her hands by 6p.m. on December 15th. The paper could be turned in early, but no student, she emphasized, would pass the course without submitting the paper by the due date. "Don't be the student with poor time management, upset at the end of the semester when their lack of discipline causes them to fail based on the choices they made," she exclaimed.

As the semester drew to a close, Brian Smith had an "A" average in Professor Jessup's class and was about to begin researching his paper topic. Brian was thought of as brilliant by his classmates, but that doesn't mean he was well liked. He took pride in raising his hand and answering questions before other students had a chance to answer. He attempted to show other students he was smarter than them, bragging about "A"s he'd earned on tests and papers while laughing at students that didn't do as well. Brian was so difficult to deal with that he had acquired the nickname "Suge Knight" in the classroom.

At home, it was a different story. Brian was a caring/thoughtful husband and father. Kim, Brian's wife, felt insecure about Brian getting his college degree. She only had a high school diploma. Adding to her insecurity, a co-worker at the bakery she worked teased her saying that Brian would one day dump her for a college girl. Kim began accusing Brian of having an affair and suggested he drop out of college. Brian did everything he could to eliminate any doubt of infidelity in her mind. He would joke about friends they knew who cheated in their marriage, and he'd hold her hand as he had talks with Kim about how seriously he took their marriage and his fidelity. Brian would speak slowly and softly in an effort to let her know he was serious. None of that helped.

Complicating the situation was the fact that Kim and Brian had a child while in high school, both still graduated but instead of going to college, they got jobs. Their son David was having problems at school, and his grades were not what they wanted them to be. David and Brian were close. Brian knew just what to say to pick him up when he was down and bring him down a notch when hubris got the best of him. So, along with convincing Kim he was not interested in any other women on a daily basis, working a full time job, and tutoring his son, Brian was taking the Philosophy course. The final paper was all that was between him and an "A".

You might call Brian's relationship with Professor Jessup tenuous at best. The professor had received five complaints about him from classmates. She had been watching him talk down to classmates in group discussions; he would thrust his hand in their faces, if he wanted them to stop talking to him. He could be aggressive and a bully. There were even a few occasions when Brian disagreed with research in the textbook and argued with the professor about the findings. Professor Jessup was not necessarily fond of Brian, but there was nowhere on her grading scale that accounted for her fondness of a student. He (as every student) would get the grade according to the points he earned.

Brian thought getting an "A" in the class was a foregone conclusion, but nothing is guaranteed. It can be hard to predict what will happen in life…

Assignment

What Makes a Competent Communicator?

1) How many communication situations are we aware of that Brian Smith has? Describe them (who do we know he communicates with)?

2) Is Brian a competent communicator in all of these situations?

3) Of the 5 characteristics of competent communicators, which do you think Brian uses well, and which do you think he doesn't use, or uses poorly in each situation?

4) Can Brian learn to be a more competent communicator? Why?

Brian Smith Accountability
Communication Competence Case Study
Part II

Three days before the paper was due, Brian had not accomplished much. He believed he was on his way to an "A" in the course, and he had other pressing issues going on in his life. After work and attending his Philosophy class, he was helping his son David with his homework every night. After that, he was worn out. Adding to it, the daily questions/accusations from Kim further exhausted him. Her friend at work continued to provoke her, saying, "All those college girls can be irresistible... any man would succumb to that type of pressure." If he came home 10 minutes late after asking Professor Jessup a question, she was sure he was cheating on her with a female classmate.

Despite working every day, taking classes, studying with David every night, and the tension at home, Brian finished the paper the night before it was due. The next day, he was mentally and physically exhausted. He went to work as usual, but when he was headed to class, he realized he left his paper at home. When he got there, he opened the door to a crying Kim. David had gotten into a fight at school that day and was suspended. She was so happy Brian was home so he could talk to him and discipline him properly. When Brian said he just came home to get his paper and go to class, Kim snapped. She felt as though he was choosing school and the other woman he had to be dating over his family. As she bolted out of the room in tears, Brian never saw her grab his car keys off the table.

Brian stood there wondering if he should go talk to Kim OR go to class, turn the paper in, then head right back home. He decided he had to run and turn that paper in. He went to grab the car keys, and they weren't on the usual end table he places them on. He frantically searched the house, but they were nowhere to be found. When he went upstairs to ask Kim if she had seen them, she yelled through the door, "Go to hell... that's where your keys are."

He thought to himself, "All I gotta do is turn this paper in. I'll be done with the class, have my "A", and then I can focus on Kim and David." Brian ran out to the bus; it was 5:30p.m., just 30 minutes before his term paper was due. He knew if a bus came quickly, he just might make it with a few minutes to spare. Panicked, Brian called Professor Jessup's office and left a message that he was having car trouble.

The bus came about 10 minutes later. At 6:15p.m. Brian saw some Philosophy classmates gleefully walking down the quad. They giggled and laughed as they saw him running toward the classroom. The classroom was empty, and the door was locked. He ran into Professor Jessup's office with his paper in hand.

The Professor said, "Sorry, Brian, you're 15 minutes late." She explained, "There are other students that didn't come to class today, or may run in here after you." Upset, Brian said she could accept the paper, multiple issues made him late and that she was trying to fail him. Prof. Jessup replied, "I don't want you or any student to fail. It's not about me. It's about your time management. If I accept your paper, it is not fair to students that turned theirs in on time. I'm sure some of them had issues and would have loved 15 more minutes to better their paper. Not to mention students that may come after you. Every student has to have an equal opportunity to succeed in my class and you're asking for an advantage others did not receive." Brian earned an "F" for the course.

Assignment

What Makes a Competent Communicator?

1. What characteristics of Competent Communicators could Brian have used to get his instrumental goals met competently?

2. Rank who is responsible for Brian getting an "F" in the class. Who has the most responsibility, who has the least or none? Include Brian, Kim, Kim's work friend, David, and Professor Jessup in your list and explain your reasoning for where you rank

After Completing This Exercise

Consider:

- What your accountability is across multiple communication situations you encounter.

- How you will use the characteristics of Competent Communicators to make assessments of your own communication situations.

3

Who Are You

What You Should Know

The Definition of Self-Concept

The Definition of Self-Esteem

The Relationship between Self-Esteem and Communication Behavior

The 4 Steps in Changing Your Self-Concept

The Number of Identities We Create

What You Should Do

Activities

- Watch the time codes from the film *Catch Me If You Can* and answer the questions that accompany them. You do not turn in the answers from *Catch Me If You Can* unless otherwise instructed.

Hybrid

- Post to the "Identity Management" discussion forum. Your 1st post (your answer to the discussion forum question) should be by Wednesday, but no later than Friday to earn points for the week. Remember to comment on other postings from at least 2 classmates by 5 p.m. on Sunday.

Reflection of the Week

Describe who you are. What adjectives would you use to describe yourself? How do you think these aspects help you form your identity?

Self-esteem is the part of the self-concept that assigns worth.

Introduction

Have you ever asked yourself the question, "Who Am I?" We tend to ask ourselves that question when we've done something we are not necessarily proud of, but those should not be our only moments of self-reflection. How we define ourselves, more specifically how we feel about those definitions, is intimately linked to our level of communication competence.

The Self-Concept

Our self-concept consists of a relatively stable set of perceptions we hold of ourselves. "Relatively" stable because our self-concept can change, but the core qualities generally remain consistent. For example, if someone considers themselves tall, that is a part of that person's self- concept, and it is relatively stable. But that doesn't tell you anything about their self-esteem, which factors more prominently in competent communication.

Self-esteem is the part of the self-concept that assigns worth. Using the previous example, if your self-concept is being tall, your self-esteem is how you feel about that quality. Our self-esteem be- gins to develop as children, and it is the people around us that highly influence how we feel about ourselves. If you are taller than those in your age group, often referred to as your reference group,

27

and your height is celebrated by those around you "Look at him; he's so great," or "Look at her; she's such a grown up", that tends to increase one's self-esteem or lead to positive self-esteem. While the opposite, people saying, "Look at him; he stands out like a sore thumb," or "Look at her; she doesn't fit in," tend to lead to a decrease or negative self-esteem.

Understanding this is vital because our self-esteem is a huge factor in how we communicate and behave. Our communication and behavior dictate how often our instrumental goals are competently met. People with low self-esteem more often communicate negatively, which leads to behaviors that won't get their instrumental goals competently met. Recall Chapter 1, our metaphysical selves (minds) lead our physical selves (behaviors). If our thoughts are negative regarding our self-esteem, we're beginning our quest of accomplishing an instrumental goal at a deficit.

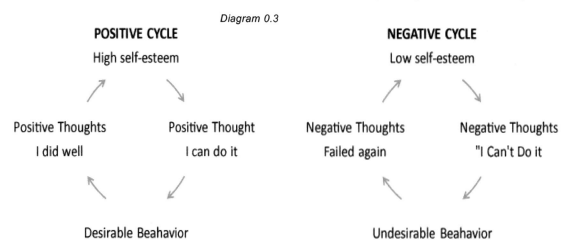

Diagram 0.3

POSITIVE CYCLE

High self-esteem

Positive Thoughts
I did well

Positive Thought
I can do it

Desirable Beahavior

NEGATIVE CYCLE

Low self-esteem

Negative Thoughts
Failed again

Negative Thoughts
"I Can't Do it

Undesirable Beahavior

Recap of Self-Concept

Our self-concepts and self-esteem are highly influenced by the feedback of our reference groups through social comparisons. If we believe we are tall, it's based on the comparison with the people around us. So being tall would be a part of our self-concept. Our self-esteem would be affected by how the reference group responds to that part of our self-concept; if there's praise for being tall, then positive self-esteem develops about height. Conversely, if teased or berated for being taller than everyone else, negative self-esteem develops about that characteristic. Negative self-esteem often leads to unachieved instrumental goals, a lack of communication competence.

So if negative relationships were attached to our self-concepts, is it possible to change our self-concept? Let's begin this conversation with an analysis of the self-fulfilling prophecy.

A self-fulfilling prophecy simply means thinking that something will happen, makes it more likely to occur. It does not guarantee it will occur; it simply makes it more likely. For example, if you're walking into an interview and you're saying to yourself, "I'm not going to do well. I'm not going to get this job," it is more likely that you won't interview well or get the job. It doesn't guarantee that you won't get the job; it just makes it less likely. Similarly, if you are saying to yourself, "I'm going to get this job; it is perfect for me," it only makes it more likely that you will interview well and get the job.

To fully understand how the self-fulfilling prophecy works, let's revisit our metaphysical versus our physical selves. The self-fulfilling prophecy extends the concept by representing a rather obvious truth: our greatest potential can be reached when combining a positive self-fulfilling prophecy with the physical preparation to achieve a goal. For instance, if you say to yourself, "I am going to do well on this test. I am not going to be nervous" (and you believe it), by using your thoughts you have created a positive self-fulfilling prophecy. If you combine that with physically studying the material over and over again, it is much more likely you'll be successful on the test.

Another possibility is; you create a positive self-fulfilling prophecy by saying to yourself, "I'm going to do well on this test" over and over again, but you haven't studied. Even with the positive self-fulfilling prophecy, you won't be very successful.

Have you ever studied really hard for a test but went into it with a negative self-fulfilling prophecy, thinking: "I didn't study enough; I'm not going to do well"? If you have, you may have been nervous while taking the test, gotten questions wrong that you knew the answers to, gone over the early questions too many times, or you were rushing to finish the test in the time allotted. A negative self-fulfilling prophecy, even when you're physically prepared for the task, can have you not reach your highest potential with that task. The key to success is to combine a positive self-fulfilling prophecy (metaphysical) with the right amount of physical preparation for any task.

The ability to create positive self-fulfilling prophecies can greatly be affected by your self-esteem. Our self-esteem plays a significant role in achieving our instrumental goals. High self-esteem leads to positive thoughts and behaviors, thus getting your instrumental goals met more often. Low self-esteem tends to lead to the opposite outcome. The question becomes: if you've attached negative thoughts to elements of your self-concept, how do you change your self-concept? The first place to start is an analysis of how to change our self-concepts.[1]

---

4 Steps in Changing Your Self-Concept

Step 1 - Realistic Perception
Generally, gaining a realistic perception of self begins with self-monitoring; i.e. re-evaluating who we are, how we communicate, and how our communication was received by others. Very important to gaining a realistic perception of self is having the right people around you that can not only tell you the great things about you, but also tell you about areas needing improvement.

Step 2- Realistic Expectations
This aspect can only be determined by you! No one can tell you what is realistic for you to accomplish and what is not. No one can comment on your self-actualization because it is up to you to accomplish (or not accomplish) your goal. Can you decide you're going to quit smoking tomorrow, and do just that? You can be sure that everything we accomplish usually begins with a positive self-fulfilling prophecy.

Step 3- Will
Again, it begins with a positive self-fulfilling prophecy; believing that you will accomplish your goal. Combining your metaphysical preparation with physical preparation makes it far more likely to accomplish whatever goal you desire.

Step 4- Skills
This means doing the research and discovering what it will take to accomplish your goal. There are many places to find the skills you need to change; including books, seminars, friends, mentors, etc.

One impediment to our success is our lack of self-knowledge. Assuming that we are a particular "way" can allow those thoughts to limit what we are able to accomplish. Taking a face-to- face Communication class may be a good example of this for some of you. If 30% of your grade is based on speaking in class and you consider yourself a "quiet" person, then you may instantly decide you can't do well. Labeling yourself as particularly "quiet" in this instance will not get your instrumental goal of getting an "A" met.

Personality Traits

Our personality traits come from two places: our genetics and the people around us. Our genes come from our parents. Therefore, we may be genetically predisposed to particular behaviors. Based on that, someone may generally be quiet more often than they're talkative. The people around us also play a large role in influencing our behavior. When we're young, they help shape our behavior by encouraging some traits and discouraging others. Experts have grouped them into 5 categories:

□

"Big 5" Traits

Extroverted	Introverted
Sociable	Reserved
Fun-loving	Somber
Talkative	Quiet
Spontaneous	Self-controlled

Agreeable	Antagonistic
Courteous	Rude
Selfless	Selfish
Trusting	Suspicious
Cooperative	Uncooperative

Open	Not Open
Imaginative	Unimaginative
Independent	Conforming
Curious	Incurious
Broad Interests	Narrow Interests

Neurotic	Stable
Worried	Calm
Vulnerable	Hardy
Self-pitying	Self-satisfied
Impatient	Patient

Conscientious	Undirected
Careful	Careless
Reliable	Undependable
Persevering	Lax
Ambitious	Aimless

What's really important to realize is that all of these traits are inside of us, just at differing degrees. We may be predisposed to use one over the other, but that doesn't mean the other is absent. That's an important realization for competent communicators because they learn when to pull out the necessary trait to get an instrumental goal met. Our "quiet" student can no longer remain that way in the classroom situation, if that person wants to be a competent communicator.

Identity & Honesty

With the knowledge that each of the personality traits exist in all of us (just at varying rates), the next step is recognizing our usage of many of these traits in creating multiple identities. In other words, we strive to create multiple identities because we realize that they are necessary to communicate competently in different situations. Think about all the identities you currently display; you may be a sister or brother, a mother or father, a mentor or a student. Your identity as a parent may require you to use different aspects of who you are to get your instrumental goals met with your children versus your identity as a student. You use different identities (or aspects of your personality) to be successful in both situations. For example, the identity you use if you have an eight-month-old baby and you're keeping them from crying would not be successful if used when you're in college taking a communications course. Creating these different identities allows us the best chance to competently get our instrumental goals met in various situations.

We can create an unlimited amount of identities to get our instrumental goals met; they vary based on the situations we find ourselves in. But there is a dark side to this. Unfortunately, we can sometimes take it too far and create false identities. False identities occur when we create images of ourselves that don't really represent who we are, our likes and dislikes, and/or our value system. A very simplistic example of this is when dating a potential mate, and we see something he/she likes or has an interest in. Acting or expressing interest in the same thing when that's not the case, can lead to future trouble in the relationship. If you've ever done this (or someone has done it to you), you know that the false identity generally has a very short shelf life. It is difficult for someone to maintain a false identity; our true selves will fight to surface.

This is why honesty in identity management is so important. If honest from the beginning, we're really protecting our competence in future interactions with the individual. In other words, it's misleading to create a false identity. When our honest identity surfaces (typically it's only a matter of time), it may be the end of getting our goals met with the other individual. Consider if at the beginning of a relationship, you claim to enjoy watching sports, when in reality you are not a sports fan. After watching and attending so many football, basketball, and baseball games, the truth will likely surface. How long can we do something we don't really enjoy? Are we hoping that by the time the other person finds out that he/she won't care? That's unlikely because carrying on a lie for a long period of time tends to make that individual question the other's character and motivation. Honesty, at the beginning, can avoid such pitfalls. Let's not forget, if people can't or don't accept you as you are, should you really want to be with them in the first place?

Key Reflections

Think about the excerpts from the film *Catch Me If You Can* you watched, and reflect on the identities you've created in the past. When some- one asks you "Who Are You", are the adjectives you use to describe yourself authentically you?

Competent communicators properly manage their identities, allowing them to achieve their goals more often. However, identity management is a collaborative process, communicated from one communicator to another. The following chapters examine the ways we communicate with others; beginning with our perception, language, and finally nonverbal communication.

Chapter Activity 3

Significant Questions: Catch Me If You Can (2002)

<u>Time Codes</u>
3:05 – 8:50
13:06 – 22:46
31:40 – 40:30
49:00 – 56:50
1:52:18 – 1:57:50
Total= 35 minutes

1. What is first identity we see Frank Abagnale Jr. create?

2. What is the second identity that Frank creates?

3. What identity does Frank create to fool FBI agent Hanratty?

4. Would you call any of the identities honest? Why or why not?

5. Choose one of Frank's identities we referred to above and describe what you believe his goal was when he created it. Also explain if he communicated competently when he used that particular identity.

6. Based on your answers, what is the problem with creating false identities in the long run?

4

How We Know

What You Should Know

The Steps in the Perception Process

The Definition of Stereotyping

How to Combat Stereotyping

The 3 Elements of Perception Checking

The Difference between Empathy and Sympathy

What You Should Do

Activities

- Watch the time codes from the film *As Good As It Gets* and answer the questions that accompany them. You do not turn in the answers from *As Good As It Gets* unless otherwise instructed.

Hybrid

- Post to the *As Good As it Gets* discussion forum. Your 1st post (your answer to the discussion forum question) should be by Wednesday, but no later than Friday to earn points for the week. Remember to comment on other postings from at least 2 classmates by 5 p.m. on Sunday.

<u>Reflection of the Week</u>
Write about a personal/professional situation when you used sympathy or empathy, and you communicated competently.

Introduction

Have you ever talked to a family member or friend about an experience you had together, and that person described the event totally different than the way you recall it? This occurs because each of us experiences a different reality that is shaped by our interests, biases, and previous experiences.

Another key element to consider is that we perceive the world using one or more of our five senses: taste, touch, smell, sight, and hearing. But these senses differ in strength, depending on the individual and may be used differently according to preference. For example, if you went to a restaurant with a friend, you may remember exactly what the food tastes like but not so much the ambiance, while another observer may better recall the restaurant's decor.

Because there is such a great gap between "what is" and "what we know", making correct interpretations can be difficult.

Finally, maybe the most important thing to consider about perception is the fact that there is a GREAT gap between "what is" and "what we know"! Using the example from the previous para- graph, what if the food was good (taste), it was warm (touch/feel), it smelled of fresh garlic (smell), the restaurant was well lit (sight), and soft jazz was playing in the background (sound)? However, you could not perceive that the food was prepared earlier that day and left out too long so it made you sick later; it was warm because it was microwaved. The garlic smell was from the bread placed on the table not your meal. The lighting was perfect because the sun was setting, but when the sun disappeared, the restaurant was too dim. The soft jazz music was from the next door neighbor's and ended when they turned it off in the middle of your meal. This demonstrates the limitations of our perception and exactly why that gap between "what is" and "what we know" is so large.

Imagine other things that happened in the restaurant that you simply could not perceive. You could say that your food was good and generally tell people it is a "good" restaurant, but what if your dish is the only good dish there? If you didn't taste anything else, the small sample size of your perception may make your assessment of the restaurant incorrect. The day you were there you perceived it as warm in the restaurant, but did you know that the air conditioner was broken that day and normally it is rather cool? Our perceptions provide only a small picture of what is really happening, and even that small picture may be accurate or inaccurate to someone else. One of the major problems in communication is that we believe our perceptions are accurate, true, and/ or universal. This problem can often lead to poor communication. A much deeper analysis of this will take place in Chapter 5 on Language.

Perception & Stereotypes

Our perceptions lead us to different understandings of what an event was, what it stood for, and what actually occurred during the event. Although it is vital to understand that our perceptions are different, how we construct our own perceptions is the focus of this chapter. The way we create understanding is called the perception process. In his book Reflect & Relate, McCornack identifies three steps: Selection, Organization and then Interpretation.1

Step 1- Selection
We are constantly bombarded with sensory information, probably more today than any other time of human existence. From television to radio and from billboards to street signs, we are inundated with information begging for our attention. Choosing to pay attention to an item or object is the first step in the perception process called selection.

Step 2- Organization
After an item is selected, the next step is to organize it in some meaningful way. Can you imagine how much different our lives would be if our brains did not organize information for us? What if every time you walked into a classroom, you couldn't identify the instructor versus the students, or classify situations as dangerous or safe? Organization is a vital function; it allows us to classify like things and avoid wasting time when introduced to items that aren't exactly alike. An example of this is in elementary school; students often sit at desks that are square, have a storage area below the top, and a separate chair. However, when making the transition to high school, those same students are sitting at desks that are attached to chairs. The high schoolers don't need to learn what those chairs are because they have the ability to categorize them as desks, similar to those they used in elementary school.

Life would be much more difficult if our brains didn't naturally organize information for us, but emanating from that function is **stereotyping**. Stereotypes are exaggerated generalizations associated with categorization. They may be based on some past experience or knowledge, and many are culturally accepted as accurate generalizations. For example, someone may hold the stereotype that elderly people drive slowly based on the fact that individual drove behind an elderly person who was driving slowly.

This actually brings us to an interesting point; stereotyping is not inherently wrong, and depending on the situation it may keep you out of harm's way. For example, if you are walking toward a man that "looks" dangerous because he's wearing a hood, not making eye contact, and his hands appear to be holding something in his pocket, crossing the street could save your life.

Two Ways We Stereotype
1. Categorizing people by identifying easily recognizable characteristics and applying a stereotype to a particular individual. An example of this occurs when people notice someone is tall and assuming that he/she plays basketball.

2. Recognizing particular characteristics and applying a stereotype to Most or All others that hare those characteristics. When people make statements like, "Women can't drive", or "Men are insensitive", they are referring to Most or All women and men. This can be very problematic when communicating because people often prefer not to be categorized, particularly in categories they perceive as negative.

Because stereotyping emanates from a natural function of the brain (organization), it is impossible to stop stereotyping. But competent communicators learn how to combat stereotyping. A competent communicator's goal is to read the communication situation accurately and produce the most appropriate behavior for the situation. As previously mentioned, there are times when the stereotype is correct, and it can lead to demonstrating a high level of communication competence. But, in most environments (like in a college classroom), competent communicators **decategorize** --they treat everyone as an individual. Once organized, the final step in the perception process is interpretation.

Step 3 - Interpretation

Because there is such a great gap between "what is" and "what we know", making correct interpretations can be difficult. When someone across the room winks at you, is that person flirting... or is something in that person's eye? When someone says "Stop by anytime", does that person literally mean anytime, or is that individual just saying it to be friendly? Our past experiences play such a huge role in how we interpret information that knowing nothing about the other communicator's past makes competent communication more difficult.

Perception Checking

Our self-concept can also play a large role in our interpretation of information. Let's say if the adjective "smart" is a part of your self-concept, creating high self-esteem. You have high grades and are often told how smart you are. What happens when people call you stupid? Likely, you would interpret it as a joke and laugh it off, thinking "That's funny, they don't even know me." But, if you believe you're unintelligent and someone calls you stupid, you are much more likely to become upset. This demonstrates a key element about interpretation: we have 100% control over how we interpret information, regardless of what is said or communicated. We have the power to control our emotions simply by how we interpret the message. Even then, there is no guarantee our perception is correct. How can we be sure our interpretation of the message is what the other communicator intended? Adler and Proctor refer to the perception checking process below as a great method to ensure correct message interpretation.[2]

Steps of Perception Checking

Step 1- The Specific Behavior

It is important to communicate exactly what was observed (in Chapter 5, it's referred to as using contextual statements) rather than making a statement of judgment regarding a general belief. For instance, if the goal was to find out why the dishes weren't done, a correct statement would be, "You didn't do the dishes last night" versus "You are lazy" or "You don't care".

Step 2 -Consider at least Two Possible Interpretations of the Behavior

This is important because by only providing one possible interpretation, it suggests that we know the reason why the other communicator behaved as they did. In reality, there is a great gap between "what is" and "what we know". It is better not to assume or seem presumptuous. In the situation above, it may be better to say, "I'm not sure if you fell asleep, or just forgot it was your turn to do the dishes, or why they aren't done." Remember, there could be many reasons why.

Step 3- Ask for Clarification

The goal is clear understanding, while at the same time keeping the other communicator from becoming defensive. To assume you know, instead of asking for clarification, sends a negative message to the other communicator. Asking for clarity allows the other communicator to feel respected as the complex individual they are.

Once there's a shared understanding of what each communicator is trying to say, competence can still be lost if they can't relate to the other's motive. This is when empathy and sympathy come back into play.

Empathy & Sympathy

Empathy is attempting to feel another's pain, while sympathy is attempting to understand from one's own perspective. They were the fourth characteristic of competent communicators in Chapter 2. What wasn't addressed then was the fact that one can never fully achieve empathy or sympathy because it's impossible to literally feel someone else's pain or completely understand exactly someone's point of view. A competent communicator attempts both, at the right time, to the best of their ability.

Another important aspect to consider is we sometimes believe our experience (or lack thereof) dictates our ability to empathize or sympathize. For instance, thinking that because someone has gone through an experience, that individual should empathize with someone else going through it. If someone has not gone through a similar circumstance, that individual can only sympathize. This is untrue. Having gone through an experience may make it easier to empathize, but we can choose to use empathy or sympathy regardless of whether or not we've had a similar experience. In movie theatres all over the world, people are empathizing and sympathizing with characters that aren't real people and with experiences that they have never had before. How many of you have cried in a movie, not because you had gone through what the character endured, but because you felt a connection with the character? If so, that was an evidence of our ability to be empathetic without having gone through the experience.

Key Reflections

After watching the excerpts from *As Good As It Gets* and answering the significant questions that accompanied the film, think about a personal or professional situation when you used sympathy or empathy. How did it aid your communication competence in that situation?

When we communicate, there's usually a pretty clear picture in our head of how we feel. We're trying to transmit that exact picture into the other communicator's brain, hoping they might see our picture just as we do. Our ability to use empathy and sympathy are vital in this effort. One of the best transmitters of information in our arsenal are words (spoken and written). They can either aid or betray us. The next chapter focuses on language: master it and allow it to foster competent communication.

Chapter Activity 4

Significant Questions: As Good As It Gets (1997)

Time Codes
0 – 10:07
10:07 – 14:35
23:24 – 35:31
58:28 – 1:02:28
1:02:28 – 1:07:21
Total= 35 minutes

1. Name Mr. Udall's (Jack Nicholson's character) first two instrumental goals. Does his communication style allow him to be a competent communicator?

2. Name the common stereotypes Mr. Udall uses and which of the two ways we stereotype (from the text) he's applying?

3. What statement do you think Mr. Udall is making regarding gender roles?

4. What psychological challenges might Mr. Udall have influencing his perception?

5. Does Mr. Udall use empathy or sympathy at any point? If you think so, when?

6. Serious problems can arise when people treat interpretations as if they were matters of fact. Write the 3 part perception check. How could Carol have used the 3 part perception check to communicate more competently with Melvin?

5

Language

Symbolism
The Power of our Words
Static Evaluations vs. Fluidity
The Responsibility Inherent in Language

What You Should Know

The Definition of Language

The Meaning of Static Evaluations

The Definition of Fluidity

The Meaning of Contextual Statements

The Difference between Denotative and Connotative Meanings

About Emotive Words

The 6 terms in the Language of Responsibility

What You Should Do

Activities

- Complete the "I" Statement exercise.

Hybrid

- Post your *"I" Statement* to the discussion forum. Your 1st post (your answer to the discussion forum question) should be by Wednesday, but no later than Friday to earn points for the week. Remember to comment on other postings from at least 2 classmates by 5p on Sunday.

Reflection of the Week
Write about a recent personal/professional interaction that didn't go well, and write the "I" statement you could have used in hopes of keeping communication open.

Introduction

Do you know people whose verbal skills are so great it seems as though they get everything that they want? They are persuasive and have a mastery of the English language that impresses others, perhaps more with their fluency than with compelling content. However, in your eyes, they choose their words so well that their ability to get their instrumental goals met seems unparalleled.

Our use of language allows us to do things that it appears other animals on the planet seem incapable of, for instance: humans can make considerations of the past and the future, pose "what if" questions, and communicate massive amounts of knowledge from generation to generation regarding a multitude of subject matters. Language, and our ability to write it down, has allowed us to prosper and grow in ways our other animal counterparts can't match. But what is language, and how does it work?

Symbolism

When considering language, there are two vital aspects that must be addressed: First, language is symbolic, meaning the letters put together for a person, place, thing, or idea only represent that because a group of people have agreed that it does.[1] Consider in English the combination of the symbols "T-R-E-E" to represent that brown thing that lives outside, sucks up carbon dioxide, and provides oxygen to the earth (to name a few things). However, in Spanish, the symbols "A-R-B-O-L" represent that same item. Which one is correct?

The second thing to consider is that these symbols are arbitrarily chosen; there is no real correlation or connection between these symbols and the items they represent. It is impossible for those few symbols to truly encompass the essence of what something is. For instance, although we can think of a number of things a "tree" does, some aspects can be forgotten. Some trees provide shade from the sun, or are brown, green, or yellow. The arbitrarily chosen symbol "T-R-E-E" has no relationship to the essence of what "it" is.

Think about it! The symbol given to something cannot really represent its essence. If this is the case, why get upset when people call us a perceived negative word outside of our names? Do we believe that the essence of us is that negative word? Recall from the Interpretation section in Chapter 4, the example of laughter being an appropriate response when someone labeled us as something that we believe to be inaccurate; the example was calling someone stupid that earned all "A's" in school. Rather than take that comment to heart and give it meaning, the individual would laugh because as far as that person is concerned it was an untrue statement. It had no power or truth. The individual, it was said, had the power to give it meaning or take it away. We all determine the power of a symbol (words) and just as easily as we give one power, we can take that power away.

When we communicate with others, where does the meaning of what we say really lie? The meanings lie in the other communicator, so your knowledge and understanding of the other person plays a major role in how well you are able to paint that picture in that individual's head, leading to competently communicate.

Imagine a high school basketball coach watching lackluster effort from his team and imploring his players to "be aggressive" in practice and in games. A few weeks into the season, a parent of one of the students pulls the coach aside and says, "Coach, I was wondering if you could stop telling the kids to be aggressive. My child doesn't like that term and finds it intimidating." The coach's instrumental goal was to get the players to play harder, and maybe he was competent with 11 out of the 12 players. To be competent with the 12th, he would have to be adroit with language and use other words to communicate competently.

From the perspective of the player, if his instrumental goal were to earn playing time, he may need to change his self-concept. If he views him- self as unaggressive or views aggressive behavior as a negative, he would need to change his self-concept to view aggressiveness as positive in particular contexts. He can also realize that all of the traits necessary for his success are inside of him; it's just a matter of using them at the appropriate time (2nd characteristic of competent communicators).

The Power of Our Words- Static Evaluations versus Fluidity

As addressed in Chapter 3, everyone has all of the Big 5 personality traits, just at varying degrees based on genetics and influenced by the people around us. Examining those traits and attempting to choose just one to describe yourself can be very difficult. Mainly because it suggests that we are constant or unchanging; this is called a static evaluation.

Static evaluations are statements like, "I am a quiet person". This suggests that you are constantly quiet. When in reality, there are likely times when you are loud. It would be much more accurate to give the statement context (or more specific detail) by saying: "I am quiet when I'm around people I don't know." Conversely, you may say: "I am loud when I'm at a sporting event." Adding context to the statement "I am quiet" paints a more accurate picture of our ever-changing nature, simply referred to as our fluidity.

This is an important realization for competent communicators. Communicating using static evaluations often leads to the other communicator becoming defensive. Defensiveness is the enemy to competent communication. Once someone becomes defensive, communication tends to cease. For example: if Communicator A notices that Communicator B didn't do the dishes when it was their turn, Communicator A may make a static evaluation and state, "You never do the dishes". Typically, Communicator B becomes defensive and a heated debate ensues about the last time they did the dishes. Due to the static evaluation, Communicator A's instrumental goal to get the dishes done is not met.

Competent communicators practice making contextual statements; these are statements that directly address the issue, topic, or behavior. In the example above, a proper contextual statement would have been: "It was your turn to do the dishes last night, and the dishes aren't done". Using contextual statements will more likely lead to competent communication than static evaluations.

The Responsibility Inherent In Language

Competent communicators have a good grasp of the deeper meanings of how particular words they say affect the other communicator. Particularly, they are not just aware of the denotative (dictionary) meanings of words but also the connotative meanings (secondary meaning of a word, regarding its associations, overtones, and/or its feeling). There are some words that carry a connotative meaning that goes beyond its denotative; they are referred to as emotive words. They can carry a positive or negative feeling, even though their dictionary meanings are similar. Examples of these include:

Positive Connotation		Negative Connotation
Urban	vs.	Inner-city
Traditional	vs.	Old-fashioned
Liberal	vs.	Radical
Thrifty	vs.	Cheap

It is important to be aware that a general connotation exists for a particular term to avoid an unintended meaning to be interpreted by the other communicator. For example, if you're shopping with someone and you are really impressed by how many items that person buys while spending a small amount of money, a compliment will likely be received well by calling them "thrifty" versus "cheap". Knowing general connotative meanings of words is a tool of competent communicators.

In addition to connotative meanings, competent communicators are also very aware of words that inherently assign responsibility. When using the term "I", we are accepting responsibility. For example, with the statement "I did not do the dishes", the speaker is accepting the responsibility for not completing the task.

"You" statements place blame. If someone says, "You did not do the dishes", that person is placing the responsibility squarely on your shoulders.

"We" statements share the responsibility. Someone might say, "We didn't get the dishes done." That suggests both parties share the blame for the incompletion of the task.

"It" statements avoid responsibility, leaving it in some ambiguous realm. If someone says, "It's unfortunate the dishes aren't done", where does the responsibility belong? Who is to blame for not doing the dishes?

Using the term "but" can add clarity to a situation, and when used properly, it can provide more detail about a situation. If someone said, "You didn't do the dishes last night, but I'm not sure if you knew it was your turn." "But" statements can help further explain your perspective and fight against the other communicator becoming defensive, when used properly.

Finally, the most powerful of the language of responsibility are "questions". Competent communicators have mastered the art of asking sincere questions because they can be the kryptonite to defensiveness. Think about the times loved ones asked sincere questions. This may have taken place after you were out late one night. Coming home and seeing the worry in their eyes and relief in their voice when they said, "I was worried about you. Where were you?" Rather than becoming defensive and shutting down communication, it's more likely you communicated to ease their anxiety.

Questions can be just as powerful in creating poor communication situations; all it takes is an insincere question. Imagine coming home and hearing a sarcastically remarked, *Where were you?*" Inherent in the way the question was posed is the belief you were doing something you shouldn't have been. The question itself can lead to an argument, not necessarily about the content, but why the question was asked in that way (paralanguage). The instrumental goal of finding out where the other communicator was goes unmet.

There is another problem with the insincere question: recall the statement in Chapter 4, *there is a great gap between "what is" and "what we know"*. Internalizing this statement as truth means that rather than assuming we know why someone else behaved in a particular way, we know we're only guessing the other's motivation or reason. Consider this: You arrived somewhere late due to a flat tire. The other communicator assumed that you were delayed due to leaving the house late, as usual. The smirk and sarcasm are apparent when they say, *"Why are you late? I shouldn't even ask because you're always late."* People making assumptions about us or static evaluations often lead to defensiveness. Competent communicators constantly remind themselves that they don't know why other people are motivated to behave as they do. The gap between "what is" and "what they know" is too great for them to assume. That perspective can lead them to ask more sincere questions.

Asking sincere questions is great, but have you ever spent a large amount of time with children from the ages of 4 to 7? Many ask questions about everything, from why is the sky blue to where babies come from? If someone is constantly asking questions, you just might want to take a break from that person. The point here is that over (or incorrect) use of any of the language of responsibility terms can be annoying to the other communicator.

All of the terms above have their drawbacks; "but" statements can be confusing to the other communicator when the second part of the statement contradicts or negates the first part. For instance, "You are a great person, but I don't want to see you anymore."

Overuse of "It" statements will never get the dishes done. If no one ever takes responsibility, then situations can go perpetually unresolved. What would happen if someone said, "We really need to get those dishes done," but the other communicator could care less if the dishes got done or not. Be sure that the responsibility is really shared, or else your instrumental goals can go unmet.

Overuse of the term "You" will make the other communicator feel as though they are to blame far too often and give the perception that the person making the statement is not responsible for anything in the relationship. Although some may feel that it's quite honorable to accept the blame in situations, the overuse of the term "I" makes people appear self-absorbed.

One key to understanding how and when to use these terms is thinking of them just as the 5 Big Personality Traits in Chapter 2. We've identified another item in your tool kit. They have always been there, but now there's a heightened awareness of them and now there's an instruction manual. It's also a matter of appropriately using each of them at the right time to communicate competently. But, what about when you feel wronged? Maybe someone has done something you didn't appreciate and a discussion has to happen. We're about to add another element to your tool kit: In their book *Looking Out, Looking In*, Adler and Proctor refer to it as the "I" statement.[2]

"I" Statements

The "I" statement is a powerful tool for the competent communicator to move away from "You" language, which can make others defensive, into language that allows for communication to continue and the possibility of competent communication.

In other words, "I" Statements are intended to be a more accurate, less offensive way of expressing a complaint versus "You" language. Think about what happens when someone says, "You're lying to me!" Unfortunately, this statement often leads to an argument, and it leaves little chance for competent communication.

What if you used an "I" statement formed in this way:

1. Your Feelings

"I am hurt right now." (or uncomfortable, confused, worried, sad, rejected, embarrassed, or abandoned). The key is to use words that make the other communicator wonder "why" and want to hear more, rather than think "It's not my fault." Often words like angry, suspicious, disgusted, puzzled, upset, or disappointed can make others defensive.

2. The Other's Specific Behavior (using contextual language) and your Interpretation

"You didn't answer the phone or call me back after I left two messages last night. I didn't know if something bad happened to you or if you just had too much to drink and were at your friend's house."

3. The Consequence (how your relationship will change if behavior continues)

"If this continues, I'm afraid that it will really damage our relationship."

"I" statements do not guarantee competent communication, but nothing can guarantee that. "I" statements may make it more likely. Remember, only you are in your relationship! You know what words trigger defensiveness in the individuals you regularly communicate with. Your ability to create conversation with the other communicator rather than defensiveness with your words will be a determining factor in achieving communication competence.

"I" Statements do not guarantee competence... but make it more likely.

Key Reflections

Think about a recent personal or professional interaction that did not go well. How could you have used an "I" Statement to communicate more competently? How will the knowledge of the responsibility inherent in language allow you to communicate more competently in future situations?

Remember that extremely persuasive individual from the beginning of this chapter? That person may have a large vocabulary and choose their words impeccably, but language can only take that person (and you) so far. Another key component to communication competence lies in nonverbal communication.

Chapter Activity 5

"I" Statement Exercise

Assignment

Visualize a situation (or create a situation) in your life when you may have sent one of these messages to someone else:

Example 1: Someone brought food home only for themselves and you said, "You think only of yourself!"

OR

Example 2: An individual is watching television, and you believe he or she is not listening to you, so you said, "You don't listen to a word I say!"

Create your own situation and an "I" statement to replace the "You" statement.

Sample

Your mate didn't call you back last night and you said, "You are so rude!"

Below is the "I" Statement to replace the "You" statement above:

"I'm feeling hurt right now. You didn't answer the phone or call me back after I left 2 messages last night. I didn't know if something bad happened to you, or if you just had too much to drink and were at your friend's house. If this continues, I'm afraid that it will really damage our relationship."

6

Nonverbal

2 Characteristics

7 Types

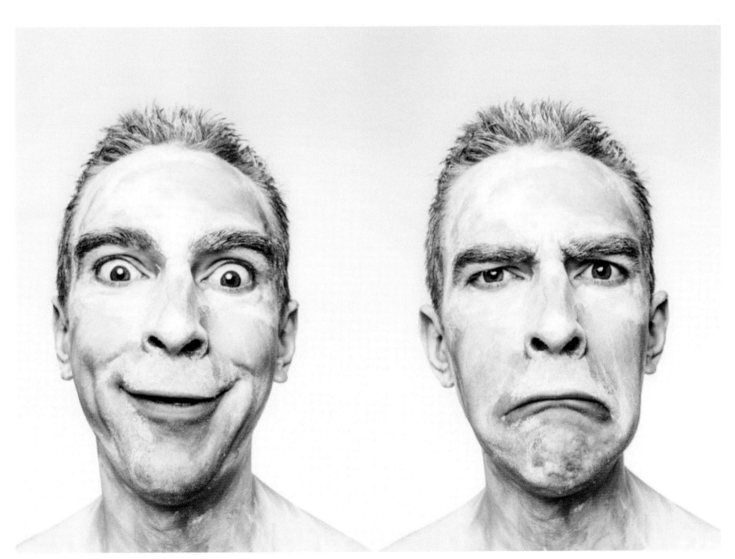

What You Should Know

The Definition of Nonverbal Communication

The Characteristics of Nonverbal Communication

The 7 Types of Nonverbal Communication

What You Should Do

Activities

- Watch the time codes from the film *Hitch* and answer the questions that accompany it. You do not turn in the answers from *Hitch* unless otherwise instructed.

Hybrid

- Post to the *Hitch* discussion forum. Your 1st post (your answer to the discussion forum question) should be by Wednesday, but no later than Friday to earn points for the week. Remember to comment on other postings from at least 2 classmates by 5 p.m. on Sunday.

Reflection of the Week

Which of the nonverbal communication types do you use well? Which will you use more often in the future to help get you communicate competently? Why?

Introduction

When talking about interpersonal communication, nonverbal communication takes center stage. Some scientists suggest that somewhere be- tween 65% and 93% of the emotional impact of a message comes through nonverbal means.[1] So first, we need to define the term.

For our purposes, nonverbal communication is any message expressed without using words. Therefore, virtually any messages sent that don't include language or the composition of words is considered nonverbal communication. Messages sent without using our vocal cords (waving, pointing, etc.) we consider nonvocal nonverbal communication. Thus, nonverbal communication that consists of vocal expressions, like sighs, laughs, cries, literally all noises made vocally that aren't words are categorized as vocal nonverbal communication.

Another interesting aspect of nonverbal communication is that it helps us define our relationships. Think about the last time you saw someone you knew and were shocked when that person reached for a hug. From your perspective, a wave while you walked by would have sufficed. But their arms stretched towards you as your outstretched fist lounged toward them for a far from intimate fist bump. They offered a hug while you didn't feel that level of intimacy with them. You were attempting to define the relationship through that nonverbal interaction. Generally speaking, the closer we perceive the person to us, the more intimate our nonverbal communication. A casual acquaintance might receive a wave and/or a verbal "hello", while a hug is reserved for someone much closer. Touching tends to play a larger role the more intimate the relationship.

Recall Chapter 1, specifically the fifth principle of communication stated that every verbal message contains words (or content) and how we feel about the other communicator (or the relational dimension). The relational dimension was a particular type of nonverbal communication called paralanguage. Paralanguage is the way something is said: its tone, speed, volume, etc. It is vocal nonverbal communication; sighs, laughs, are examples of behavior that fall in this category. It comes through our vocal cords, but those sounds do not create words. This is considered vocal nonverbal communication.

Two Characteristics of Nonverbal Communication

Adler and Proctor note characteristics of nonverbal communication that are important for analysis.[2]

□
Characteristic 1: Continuous

Have you ever spent a significant amount of time with small children? Sometimes, when they get angry, they decide they are not going to communicate anymore. They stop talking, go to the back of the room, fold their arms and pout while facing the wall. Did their ploy work? Or do you interpret their nonverbal behavior to mean that they are upset about something? All behavior has communicative value; meaning every- thing we do lends itself to interpretation. But how reliable are those interpretations?

□
Characteristic 2: Uncertain

Imagine you're spending time with a generally talkative friend, but this day, that person is silent. Generally, your first assumption may be that there is something wrong, but let's consider a number of possibilities: they are sleepy, hungry, thinking about their date last night, no longer want to share with you, we could go on and on. Because of the great gap between "what is" and "what we know", assuming knowledge of why people choose to behave as they do can lead to defensiveness in them. The ambiguous nature of nonverbal communication combined with the emotional importance of nonverbal communication (65%-93%) compels competent communicators to not assume they know its meaning. As referred to in Chapter 5, it's wiser to ask sincere questions.

Many authors, like Floyd in her book <u>Interpersonal Communication: The Whole Story</u>, have noted many types of nonverbal communication.[3] Here, we'll sum them up and focus on seven.

Seven Types of Nonverbal Communication

1. Body Movement - This category contains what is thought of as the easiest and most difficult of the types of nonverbal communications to decode. Body movement can be broken down into four categories: body orientation, posture, gestures, face, and eyes.

Body orientation refers to the level to which we're facing the other communicator. There are body orientation expectations depending on how serious the conversation. If it's serious, we expect the other's body, feet, and most importantly head to be directed toward ours. Has someone ever began a conversation while you were watching something you wanted to see on television, and that person walked right in front of the television set to demonstrate just how important it is to him or her (and should be to you)? This is an example of how important body orientation is to communication. It is also important to note that this, as well as many, of the other nonverbal communications can vary by culture, city, region, and state.

Posture, whether it is the slumping of shoulders or standing as tall as possible, is considered the easiest nonverbal communications to decode. Think about a one-on-one interview; without either party speaking, it's generally easy to tell the difference between the interviewer and the interviewee simply by looking at their posture. The interviewer generally has a more relaxed posture, while the interviewee tends to maintain a rigid or stiff posture.

Gestures are the movement of our hands and arms. Can you think of people you know that never speak with their hands or arms? Probably not! It's more likely that you know people that use too many gestures versus too few. Meaning is gathered from gestures. Others may demonstrate excitement by moving their hands fast, or if upset, they may extend their palms into another's face to signal that person to stop talking.

Face and eyes are generally considered the most difficult to decode. Facial expressions occur in- credibly fast and can be very hard to understand. It can be very hard for an individual to deter- mine exactly what the "look" someone else has on his or her face means. One person might say someone was "mean-mugging" (interpreted as making a threatening stare), while another communicator might think that individual was flirting. We also have micro expressions, which can occur and disappear so quickly, they need to be recorded and replayed in slow motion to be seen.

2. Voice - Paralanguage, as referred to in Chapter 1 and at the beginning of this chapter, is how we say words. Remember, it falls in the category of vocal nonverbal communication.

3. *Touch* - As mentioned earlier in this chapter, we define our relationships through nonverbal communication; specifically appropriate touch plays a great role in this. We shake hands with acquaintances, may hug friends, and kiss loved ones. These suggest a correlation between depth of the relationship and the intimate levels of touching. Research suggests that waiters, waitresses, and bartender's tips increase when they appropriately touch their customers.[4] Recall in Chapter 1 that the quality of our communication, which includes touch, greatly affects our health.

4. *Appearance* - This category includes clothing and physical attractiveness. Our clothing sends messages, sometimes intended and sometimes unintended. These messages can be misunderstood because other people's interpretations are heavily based on their past experiences. For example, someone can see something you're wearing. You may think it is trendy and cool, while they recall their grandmother wearing it and think it is out of style.

Our attire sends messages about us before any words are spoken. We wear, and in some cases such as school or work are forced to dress, for particular occasions to send specific messages. Appropriate dress differs based on the occasion. For instance, you probably wouldn't wear a suit to most religious ceremonies or sporting events.

Physical attractiveness can also play a large role in communicating messages. We've all probably identified successful individuals that seem to not have any particular talent. They aren't professional athletes or musicians, haven't graduated from Stanford or Harvard. Their success appears to be based on their physical attractiveness. Can you think of people at work or school that aren't the best employees or students, but seem to get advantages based on their physical attractiveness?

Some scientist suggest that somewhere between 65% and 93% of the emotional impact of a message comes through nonverbal means.

5. *Physical Space* (or Proxemics) - This category refers to the way we use space. Recall how our relationships can be defined by the level of touch? The same can be said about distance. Generally speaking, the fonder we are of someone, the more that person is allowed into our personal space. What's interesting about this topic is that physical space can vary based on cultural, city, or even neighborhood preferences. For example, if you're visiting New York City, the closeness of people as they walk down the street or ride on the subway may be shocking. Generally speaking, people pile on top of each other without a second thought. While in San Francisco, riders at the bus terminal kindly wait in a single-file line for the bus to arrive and enter according to the time they got there.

We also communicate through our territories, whether they actually belong to us or not. Our homes, apartments, and rooms may belong to us at least temporarily, yet they communicate many things about us, such as our level of cleanliness, desire for order, and our connection to others (pictures). Think about other spaces, whether temporary or not, that make statements about us; like a particular preferred seat on a bus or in a classroom. All of these are communicating ambiguous messages about us for the other communicator to decode. Pay close attention to the scene in Hitch featuring Chip, Sara, and Hitch.

6. _Physical Environment_ - This refers to how we've crafted the areas we maintain. Although few build or design the buildings in which they work or live, staging and manipulating (to some degree) those areas is almost universal. Whatever space is considered ours is shifted to pro- duce the most confirming environment as determined by us. Maybe the computer needs to move more to the left or the chair elevated and reclined. When others enter, our interior design choices have spoken, without one single word from us.

7. _Time_ - This refers to the importance of time or how it is valued. If you tell some friends to come by at 7 p.m., do you expect them to be there at 7 p.m.? Is it okay if they come late at 7:30 p.m., but not okay if they show up at 6:45 p.m.? The manner in which we treat time communicates a message to the other communicator. But our understanding of the correct usage of time varies by
situation, by region, and/or culture. For example, a lax 7 p.m. meeting time for your friends may work well for everyone, while the 11a.m. start time for a class you've enrolled in may not be flexible at all. The topic of cultural differences is further examined in Chapter 11.

Key Reflections

After watching the excerpts of _Hitch_ and answering the significant questions that accompanied the film, conduct a nonverbal self-assessment. Think about which of the seven ways we communicate nonverbally you use well and which you will improve.

U nderstanding the intentional and unintentional messages our nonverbal communication may be transmitting is a critical part of self-analysis. The next few chapters focus on topics where there is no ambiguity and are naturally intentional: self-disclosure, listening, and conflict.

Chapter Activity 6

Significant Questions: Hitch (2005)

Time Codes
  0 – 6:42
14:54 – 19:19
25:50 – 30:05
1:23:34 – 1:28:00
Total= 21minutes

1. How much of the impact of a message comes through nonverbal communication according to Hitch versus what is written in the textbook reading?

2. Write 2 examples of static evaluations (unchanging) from the film?

3. Do the statements made about "touch" support or oppose what you read in the text?

4. Describe what Albert is wearing and his body movements, when he and Hitch first meet (use contextual statements). What are those elements suggesting about Albert?

5. How does Hitch interpret Sara's nonverbal communication when they first meet, specifically what does Hitch say? (Pay attention, he uses contextual statements to describe her nonverbal communication, before he makes a judgment)

6. Using contextual statements, analyze the nonverbal communication between Hitch and Sara at his apartment?

7

Self-Disclosure

Benefits

Depth & Breadth

What You Should Know

The Definition of Self-Disclosure

The 3 Benefits of Self-Disclosure

The Definitions of Depth and Breadth in the context of Self-Disclosure

What You Should Do

Activities

- Watch the film *Full Disclosure* and answer the questions that accompany it. You do not turn in the answers from *Full Disclosure* unless otherwise instructed.

Hybrid

- Post to the *Full Disclosure* discussion forum. Your 1st post (your answer to the discussion forum question) should be by Wednesday, but no later than Friday to earn points for the week. Remember to comment on other postings from at least 2 classmates by 5 p.m. on Sunday.

Reflection of the Week
Describe a situation when you used one of the benefits of self-disclosure successfully with another communicator.

Introduction

The information we reveal about ourselves can be a great determiner of how close or distant our relationship is with the other person. Self- disclosure is the process of intentionally revealing unknown information about yourself that you deem significant. If the information is al- ready known, it is not considered self-disclosure. Revealing significant information accidentally is not considered self-disclosure either. To be considered self-disclosure the information must be unknown, significant, and it must be intentionally revealed.

Benefits of Self-Disclosure

Self-disclosure can occur for a number of reasons. For our purposes, we're going to look at three benefits of self-disclosure: reciprocity, catharsis, and self-clarification.[1]

Reciprocity- When we are motivated to disclose unknown and significant information about ourselves because another communicator has done so, it's referred to as reciprocity. In other words, it's one's honesty making the other feel comfortable or even obligated to match.

Catharsis occurs when someone has self-disclosure on his/her mind and reveals it in an effort to relieve the pressure or stress of holding it in. A common expression that encapsulates this is "getting something off your chest".

Self-Clarification tends to be used throughout relationships. Discussions about politics, love, religion, and many other topics often require it. Simply stating one's political affiliation tends not to be enough. The need to clarify our thoughts, attitudes, and feelings during self-disclosure can be spurred on by the other communicator's desire to know more. Inherent in the concept of self-clarification is the fact that we are going in depth about ourselves.

This leads us to a discussion about depth and breadth in the context of self-disclosure.

Breadth & Depth

Breadth and depth play significant roles in our relationships. Breadth in the context of self-disclosure refers to volunteering one's attitude regarding a multitude of subjects. Breadth is often used with strangers or individuals we've just met. Someone may reveal their political affiliation, favorite sport, or restaurant. It tends to be rather surface information compared to depth.

Depth refers to volunteering rather personal information about yourself. One sign of a relationship getting closer is the level of depth the conversation enters into with the other communicator. More detail is provided about ourselves, specifically why we are the way we are. Think about your relationships and rank them based on the closeness you feel to individuals. Then think of the depth of self-disclosure in each relationship. It's likely that a correlation exists between those at the top of the list and a greater level of self-disclosure.

However, we've all known people we thought bucked the trend and self-disclosed too much information far too early in relationships. To us, they were letting people in too soon, before the other communicator had earned enough trust. Casual relationships stay at the surface. More intimate relationships have a combination of breadth and depth. Awareness of appropriate levels of self- disclosure can be important to competent communication.

Key Reflections

After watching the short film *Full Disclosure* and answering the significant questions that accompanied the film, think about how you use self-disclosure in your relationships. Based on what you've learned from the reading, are there ways you will change how and when you self-disclose information to be a more competent communicator?

As important as self-disclosure is, it is irrelevant if the other communicator isn't listening. When communicating with others, listening should take center stage as it does in Chapter 8.

Chapter Activity 7

Significant Questions: Full Disclosure (2006)

Short Film
Starring: Judy Green & Brent Sexton
Writer/Director: Douglas Horn
Previously on ITunes and segments on YouTube listed as "My Last Date"
Total = 17:57 minutes

1. Give 3 examples of the breadth of self-disclosure topics they discuss.

2. Give 3 examples of self-disclosure topics where they use depth.

3. Give 2 examples of when either communicator is using reciprocity.

4. Give 1 example of when either communicator is using catharsis.

5. Give 1 example of when either communicator is using self-clarification.

6. Do you think full disclosure will work on a first date? Why or Why not?

8

Listening

5 Step Process
4 Techniques to Listen Better

What You Should Know

How Much Time Students and People at Work Spend Listening

The 5 Steps in the Listening Process

The 4 Techniques to Listen Better

What You Should Do

Activities

- Participate in Listening classroom activity.

Hybrid

- Read and/or listen to the Center for Creative Leadership podcast on active listening. Post to the *Listening* discussion forum discussion forum.   Your 1st post (your answer to the discussion forum question) should be by Wednesday, but no later than Friday to earn points for the week. Remember to comment on other postings from at least 2 classmates by 5 p.m. on Sunday.

Reflection of the Week

Which of the 4 techniques to listen better do you do well, and which do you need to practice to get better?

Introduction

Do you remember the four tools of communication from Chapter 1? If not, they were reading, writing, speaking, and listening. All of them are important, but which one do you think is more important than the others? Research tells us that college students spend 53% of their time listening. When at work, people spend 60% of their time listening.[1] This leaves reading, writing, and speaking the remaining 47% for college students and 40% for those at work. I'm sure, judging by the name of this chapter, you knew the answer was listening.

An Analysis of Listening

In their book, Interpersonal Communications: Relating to Others, Steven and Susan Beebe describe listening as a process of creating meaning from other's spoken messages.[2] We tend to do two types of listening: mindless and mindful.

With all of the things that grab our attention-- cellphones, televisions, video games (to name a few)--listening can be a tough task. We probably use more mindless listening than any other time in human history due to these technologies. Mindless listening can also be referred to as superficial listening. It uses less energy and is used more often than mindful listening.

While mindful listening requires turning off electronics and providing full attention, it tends to occur based on the importance of the subject matter. It also requires a concerted effort to shut down internal noises as well. However, as our distractions grow, mindful listening seems to have been replaced by texts and emails. Those, by the way, can be considered inferior forms of communication because they lack the relational dimension. Although emoticons try and substitute, they really aren't comparable to the tone, inflection, and volume of the human voice.

The Listening Process

In the U.S., we have a habit of asking people the question, "Did you hear me?" In reality, hearing is just the first step in a 5-step listening process described by Adler and Proctor.[3]

Step 1 - Hearing
Hearing is the physiological process of sound waves hitting the ear drum. More than likely, when people ask the aforementioned question, the answer can almost always be "Yes." That simply means the sound waves hit your eardrum. But, that's not what the other communicator really means.

Step 2 - Attending

The next step in the process is called attending. Countless sounds may be hitting the ear drum, so a choice must be made regarding which sounds to pay attention to. Reminiscent to the first step in the perception process, the world offers us much more than we are capable of processing at one time.

Step 3 - Understanding

Understanding is the step where we make sense of the sound(s) we've selected. Many take this for granted, forgetting how often we hear and attend to a message but still don't understand it.

Step 4 - Responding

Responding, the fourth step, is crucial to competent communication. Just think of how many times you were in a conversation with someone and asked "Did you hear me?" or "Are you listening?" The question is often based on your perception of a lack of response from the other communicator. Recall, nonverbal communication is continuous. We tend to want eye contact, or the nod of a head, or a smile to signify the other communicator is listening. Our responses are more often nonverbal than verbal.

Step 5 - Remembering

Carefully following steps 1 through 4 and giving no effort towards achieving step 5, remembering, makes the first 4 steps useless. Remembering things from a conversation encourages competent communication. Think about how special you may have felt when someone remembered advice you provided long ago. It tends to create a positive communication climate, making competent communication more likely.

However, there is a serious physiological impediment to effective listening: research tells us most people forget 50% of what they hear right after hearing it. Eight hours later, it drops down to 35% remembered. Two months later, 25% is all that remains.[4] That said, thankfully, there are ways to improve our listening skills.

Techniques to Listen Better

Listening is not an easy process, but there are techniques that can help us improve our listening:

Talk less - It is very difficult to learn when you're speaking. When attempting to achieve an instrumental goal, the more information you know the better prepared you are to communicate competently. Learning and providing what the other communicator needs is vital to maintaining or enhancing the relationship. Talking less and listening more benefits that aim.

Don't prejudge – We're probably all guilty of interrupting someone because we believe we already know what that person is going to say. This can occur more often with people we've communicated with for a long time. Most prefer not to be interrupted or judged before completing a thought. Due to the great gap between "what is" and "what we know", prejudging is not a friend of competent communication.

Get rid of distractions- With the proliferation of television, cellphones, and the Internet, this era is littered with distractions. Competent communicators know when it's time to use mindless or mindful listening. When mindfully listening, it's important to get rid of distractions.

Look for key ideas- Competent communicators are excellent at listening for key ideas. Humans are capable of understanding up to 600 words per minute; however, we can only speak 100 to 150 words per minute.[5] Our brains have so much extra time to wander, focusing and identifying key points or the main theme of the communication interaction is important.

Key Reflections

Think about the elements of the listening process. Of the 4 ways to improve our listening skills, which do you do well, and which will you be practicing to increase your communication competence?

Listening is vital to competent communication. People who listen well can have an advantage over those who don't. Good listeners have more opportunities to learn information about the other communicator and identify areas of their shared environment. This is especially helpful when resolving conflicts, our topic for Chapter 9.

Chapter Activity 8

Listening Exercise

Assignment

Active Listening is a very difficult process; it takes a large amount of energy and skill! How well do you listen?

After you receive the message, do not talk to anyone!

Write down exactly what was said to you, below:

Write down what the 1st person in your group says:

Write down what the last person in your group says:

Where do you think the message was lost? What can you do as an individual to ensure you don't lose the essence of the message?

9

Conflict

The Nature of Conflict
5 Conflict Resolution Styles
6 Steps to Win-Win Solutions

What You Should Know

The Definition of Conflict

The 5 Conflict Resolution Styles

The 6 Steps to Negotiating a Win-Win Resolution

The 3 Reasons why Win-Win Situations can't be Implemented

What You Should Do

Activities

- Watch the *Conflict Resolution* episode of the television show *The Office* and answer the questions that accompany it. You do not turn in your answers unless otherwise instructed.

Hybrid

- Post to "*The Office- Conflict Resolution*" discussion forum. Your 1st post (your answer to the discussion forum question) should be by Wednesday, but no later than Friday to earn points for the week. Remember to comment on other postings from at least 2 classmates by 5 p.m. on Sunday.

<u>Reflection of the Week</u>
Describe a personal/professional situation where using a different conflict style may have allowed you to communicate competently.

Introduction

When considering conflict, the first realization to note is that conflict is natural. It literally occurs in every relationship of depth. However, conflict is not defined by major disagreements. To the contrary, a conflict could be something as simple as one person's desire to see a particular movie, and the other communicator's desire to go to another. That can be considered a conflict. In fact, Adler and Proctor assign multiple elements to the definition of conflict.[1]

A. Both parties are aware

B. Have different goals

C. Believe only one can get what they want

D. Feel dependent on each other

E. One's actions would keep (or are keeping) the other from achieving their goal

This definition provides a clearer picture of the nature of conflict. For competent communicators, resolving conflicts becomes beneficial to the relationships because they know more about the other person and how to communicate with him or her more competently the next time the situation occurs.

But how are conflicts resolved? Do we always use the same methods or strategies? Thankfully, there are multiple different means of resolving conflict. Devito notes a number of those styles in his book, The Interpersonal Communications Book.[2]

Conflict Resolution Styles

Avoiding

Often occurs due to people's apprehension to conflict. It's considered a lose-lose situation because the relationship is not allowed to grow or progress when the conflict isn't addressed. Avoiding may temporarily allow the relationship to be peaceful but can lead to dissatisfaction for the person continually avoiding conflicts.

Some people prefer to compete... Sometimes Win-Win is impossible... Sometimes people are unaware it is an option.

Accommodating

Occurs when Communicator A is passive about getting their own way but allows Communicator B to get what he or she wants. This is considered a lose-win situation because you are not getting your way, while the other person is getting their goal met.

Competing

Occurs when a person seeks their desired end, when it is in opposition to the other communicator's. It is considered a win-lose situation that can later turn into a lose-lose situation because when we compete and someone wins, often the loser is emotionally broken. The relation- ship is not maintained or enhanced, and the next time the winner has an instrumental goal to be met that person finds the relationship has changed, thus the spiral to lose-lose.

Compromising

Occurs when both parties get some of what they want but are forced to give up part of their goal. It is considered a partial lose-lose situation because a win suggests that an individual got exactly what they wanted.

Collaborating

Occurs when both parties get what they want and is considered a win-win situation. The most interesting aspect of collaboration is that when successful, it changes the nature of the conflict. Remember part two of the definition of conflict: the parties have different goals. In collaboration, the parties create a shared goal rather than maintaining individual goals. Adler and Proctor note **6 steps** in creating win-win situations:[3]

1. Identify the problem or unmet need

2. Make a date to address it with the other communicator

3. Describe the problem and/or needs

4. Consider the other communicator's point of view

5. Negotiate a solution

6. Follow up to see if the solution is working for both parties

It is important to note (as discussed in Chapter 5 in the Responsibility Inherent in Language section), overuse of any of the conflict styles will lead to communication problems in the relationship. The conflict resolution styles represent more items in your communication tool kit. Competent communicators use them all as the situation calls for them or effectively employ the old adage "pick your battles"; don't compete over everything.

Ideally, wouldn't it be great if we could collaborate to resolve every conflict, allowing both parties to win? Maybe to some, but there are a number of reasons why we can't use win-win all the time:

 ❖ Some people prefer to compete: Most of us know people who simply want to win every conflict; and to make it worse, they may want you to lose every conflict. Not to restate the obvious, but it takes both parties to collaborate, and if only one is interested, then collaboration is impossible.

❖ Sometimes it is impossible: In certain situations, like war and some sports, there is going to be a loser and a winner (although some legitimately argue there are no winners in war). Millions of people tune in to watch the Super bowl every year, and there will be one champion crowned that night.

❖ Sometimes people are unaware: Often, people do not realize that a resolution exists where both parties are able to get what they want.

Key Reflections

After watching the episode of *The Office* and answering the significant questions that accompany the film, think about personal and professional situations where using different conflict styles helped you communicate competently.

It is quite normal to be conflict averse. However, as we learned earlier in this chapter, there is no way to avoid it. So it's important when communicating with others that you manage the conflict according to your desire to be competent. We have talked a great deal about increasing your communication competence. Our focus shifts to creating positive communication outcomes. Chapter 10 attempts to put what you've learned so far to good use by applying it to a more over-arching theme.

Chapter Activity 9

Significant Questions: The Office

<u>Season / Episode</u>
2 / Conflict Resolution

1. Write the difference between the 5 conflict styles listed in the text, and those mentioned in *The Office*.

2. What is the initial dispute about, and what language of responsibility does Michael suggest they use, and what language does he suggest they NOT use?

3. What do you notice about their nonverbal communication? What does Dwight say about smiling?

4. Are any of the workers passive aggressive, if so, what examples can you name?

5. Were any conflicts resolved, if so, which ones?

6. What are the proper (6) steps to approach Win-Win situations?

10
Communication Climates

Confirming & Disconfirming Messages
Defensiveness

What You Should Know

The Definition of Communication Climate

The 3 Confirming Messages

The 9 Disconfirming Messages

The 3 Types of Defensive Mechanisms

What You Should Do

Activities

- Watch the *Vocal Discord* episode of the television show *The King of Queens* and answer the questions that accompany it. You do not turn in your answers unless otherwise instructed.

Hybrid

- Post to "*The King of Queens- Vocal Discord*" discussion forum. Your 1st post (your answer to the discussion forum question) should be by Wednesday, but no later than Friday to earn points for the week. Remember to comment on other postings from at least 2 classmates by 5 p.m. on Sunday.

Reflection of the Week

Beyond the 3 Confirming Messages listed in the textbook, list any other verbal and/or nonverbal messages that make an environment confirming for you.

Introduction

The last three chapters of the book focus on creating positive outcomes in your communications, and to a great degree, represent the confluence of a number of things from the first 9 chapters. The focus of this chapter is creating communication climates.

Every relationship has a communication climate; it's described by Adler and Proctor as the overall emotional tone of a relationship.[1] Think about it like the weather; everyone can agree on its temperature, but how it "feels" is individually based. For example, there might be a 65 degree day, which everyone in a group would acknowledge is the case simply by looking at a thermometer. However, if you were to ask how it felt outside, one person might say it's cool, another might say it's warm, yet another might say it's perfectly comfortable.

Similarly, students in a classroom can agree that there is an "open" communication environment, meaning everyone has the opportunity to speak and volunteer their ideas. But, if asked how they felt about the environment, positive and negative responses are often the norm.

The better you know someone the easier it is to create positive communication climates, similar to self-esteem in Chapter 3. The more positive the communication climate the more likely competent communication is to occur.

So where do communication climates come from? Thinking back to Chapter 6, nonverbal communication represents 65% to 93% of the emotional impact of a message. Recall from Chapter 1 that everything we say contains words (or content) and paralanguage (relational dimension/ nonverbal); it becomes clear that our nonverbal communication is largely responsible for the climate.

Yet there is another element to consider. Also in Chapter 1, the fourth principle of communication stated that the meanings of messages reside in the other communicator. It's an individual's relationship with the words (connotative meanings) that often generate their reaction. The communication climate is definitely affected by the other communicator's past experiences, not just with the words used, but people or situations one deems as similar.

Thankfully, there are some standard practices that competent communicators use to create positive communication climates. It starts with sending confirming messages.

Confirming & Disconfirming Messages

Creating a confirming communication climate cannot be overrated; research suggests it is the best predictor of marital satisfaction. Satisfied couples communicate at a 5 to 1 positive to negative statements, while dissatisfied couples are 1 to 1.[2] This isn't to suggest that it's only important to married couples. There is a strong correlation between creating positive communication climates and relational satisfaction in general, whether it is in the workplace, in the classroom, or at home. Adler and Proctor extensively identify the levels of confirming and disconfirming climates as well as our defensive tendencies.[3]

Confirming Messages

Our level of involvement and energy increases at every tier when sending confirming messages. The first level is recognition, the second acknowledgement, and the third endorsement.

□
1. Recognition

The simplest way to use recognition is by making eye contact with the other communicator. If you've ever had to discipline a child, there may have been a time when they broke eye contact and you demanded, "Look at me". The child was sending a disconfirming message suggesting they were not paying attention. Your request for eye contact was a request for recognition.

□
2. Acknowledgement

We show acknowledgement by listening to the other communicator. Recall in Chapter 8 how vital listening is to communication competence. In addition to gaining information (or knowledge) from listening, it also helps create confirming climates.

□
3. Endorsement

This may be the trickiest of the three because generally endorsement refers to agreeing with someone. Endorsement in the context of communication competence means demonstrating respect for the other communicator but not necessarily agreement.

There are no guarantees of success in all situations, but think of this material as general rules and guidelines, that make competent communication more likely. To improve your chances even more, let's take a look at how to avoid disconfirming climates, which cause others to become defensive, resulting in less competent communication.

Disconfirming Messages

There are many ways to send disconfirming messages. Competent communicators are aware of:

1. Impervious Responses - When we ignore the other communicator.

2. Verbal Abuse - Which can cause psychological pain to the other communicator.

3. Generalized Complaining

4. Interrupting

5. Irrelevant Responses – Comments do not relate to the topic being discussed.

6. Tangential Responses - Uses others' remarks to start a different conversation.

7. Impersonal Response - When we don't really respond; use of clichés.

8. Ambiguous Response - Contains messages with more than one meaning (Confusing).

9. Incongruous Response - Contains two messages that contradict each other.

Defensiveness

Defensiveness is the enemy to competent communication. So let's take a look at the defensive mechanisms and the type of language that can avoid and/or combat defensiveness. Here are 3 types of defensive mechanisms:

- Attacking the other Communicator

- Altering Important Information

- Evading the person or situation

In an effort to prevent others from becoming offended, let's refer back to Chapter 5 where Language was the central topic. Avoiding static evaluations (labeling people as unchanging) by using contextual language can aid in the other communicator becoming defensive. Rather than responding to someone's comment by stating "You're crazy", you might respond "I don't understand how you came to that conclusion."

This chapter involves the melding of multiple concepts throughout the text. It's the communication climate that sets the tone in many of our relationships; therefore it is a combination of many of the chapters. Having the desire to do so, openness to self-analysis, willingness to experiment, and disciple to implement into your daily life is vital to creating positive communication climates.

Key Reflections

After watching the episode of *The King of Queens* and answering the significant questions that accompany the show, beyond the 3 confirming messages listed in the chapter, think about other verbal and nonverbal messages that help create confirming communication climates for you.

A competent communicator's goal is to create confirming climates in order to achieve positive communication outcomes…. at least in low- context cultures. But, what about creating confirming climates with those that are high-context communicators? An analysis of Intercultural Communication is next.

Chapter Activity 10

Significant Questions: The King of Queens

Season / Episode
8 / Vocal Discord

1. Write a negative nonvocal nonverbal communication and a negative vocal nonverbal cue that Doug sends to Carrie and vice versa.

2. Write the "I" Statement that Carrie should have used during the scene in the kitchen when she doesn't want Doug to leave.

3. Describe (using contextual statements) at least 2 examples of when Doug and Carrie send confirming messages.

4. Describe (using contextual statements) at least 2 examples of when Doug and Carrie send disconfirming messages.

5. What reference is made to the ratio of 5:1 positive to negative statements? What does that comment suggest about their relationship?

6. Do Doug and Carrie use sympathy or empathy when they communicate with each other? If so, when?

7. How would you describe the climate of their relationship? Based on what you've learned in this chapter (and the entire semester), what steps can they take to communicate (thus make their relationship) better?

11

Intercultural
Communication

Ethnocentrism
Low-Context Communication
High-Context Communication

What You Should Know

The Definition of Ethnocentrism

The Aspects of Low-Context Communication

The Aspects of High-Context Communication

What You Should Do

Activities

- Participate in the Intercultural classroom activity. Do not turn in your answers unless otherwise instructed.

Hybrid

- Bypass this chapter. Not addressed in Hybrid course

<u>Reflection of the Week</u>
Beyond the 3 Confirming Messages listed in the textbook, list any other verbal and/or nonverbal messages that make an environment confirming for you.

Introduction

Communicating with others can be a difficult process even when you've grown up speaking the same language in the same house, neighbor- hood, city, state, or country. But communication becomes even more complicated when you're trying to get your message across to someone from a different country and English may not be that person's first or second language. However, as the Internet is making the world "smaller", it is important that an effort is made to learn how to communicate competently in intercultural situations.

Considerations When Communicating with other Cultures

For our purposes, think of culture as a learned system of thought and behavior that belongs to and typifies a relatively large group of people. It includes their shared beliefs, values and practices. The greatest obstacle to competent intercultural communication could be ethnocentrism. Ethnocentrism is the belief that one's culture is superior to others. To become competent communicators, recognizing differences rather than applying judgments is important. Taking concepts from previous chapters into consideration, it shouldn't be so difficult to apply them in intercultural contexts.

Recall in Chapter 5, language is a system of arbitrarily chosen symbols. To even begin the study of intercultural communication, remember that ALL languages lack the ability to express the essence of whatever it symbolizes. The English meaning of the letters T-R-E-E in no way captures the complexity of what the living object does or how it is used than the Spanish letters A-R-B-O-L. Trees: absorb carbon dioxide while creating oxygen, provide homes for insects and animals, provide hundreds of food products (fruit, nuts, syrup, etc.), just to name a few characteristics. Those randomly chosen letters in no way capture what the essence of that living object. As established in Chapter 5, it just takes a group of people to agree that those symbols represent that thing, object, or person.

Remember reading in Chapter 6 that 65% to 93% of the emotional impact of a message comes through nonverbal means. In the context of intercultural communication, understanding how different cultures use nonverbal communication may be the key to competent intercultural communication. Anthropologist Edward Hall identified two distinct ways cultures communicate; there's the Low-Context communication style and the High-Context communication style.[1] Hall was even more specific because he tied these communication styles to particular continents, countries, and nation states.

Low-context communicators look for the meaning of a message in the words (Remember Chapter 1 and the 5th Principle of Communication that includes understanding the content dimension?), while high-context communicators look for the meaning of messages from nonverbal cues (recall the relational dimension or paralanguage from Principle 5). The study and proper use of these differences is essential for successful intercultural communication. The chart below lists important differences in the communication styles:

High-Context	vs.	Low- Context
Indirect		Direct
Elaborate		Specific
Group identity		Individual identity
Group harmony (saving		Individual correctness
Silence admired		Silence is often
Elaborate, ambiguous speech		Clear, eloquent speech

In cultures that use high-context communication, members tend to talk around a point. Low-context communication cultures tend to appreciate directness, i.e. addressing the issue head-on. High-context communicators can be elaborative when they talk. They tend to use speech as an art-form, painting what can be vague pictures with words. While low-context communicators can be extremely specific; they get to the point and move on. High-context cultures often identify themselves as part of their group. Babies are given multiple names that trace them back to their specific lineage, linking them to their ethnic/genetic group. In low-context communication cultures, being an individual is key. Although links to larger groups exist, like one's nuclear family, plus aunts, uncles, and cousins, one's individual identity is paramount. People in low-context communication cultures do not include their lineage when they introduce themselves.

Group harmony is very important in high-context communication. Saving the other communicator from embarrassment is key; this one act is viewed as helping to maintain group harmony. In low-context cultures, being "right" is much more valued. The focus is not on the other communicator being embarrassed but on which person was correct in the situation. Silence represents a form of respect in high-context communication, while silence can be quite uncomfortable in a low-context culture. Elaborate speech that may talk around the point is appreciated in high-context cultures. Low-context cultures prefer clear and precise speech.

Which category would the U.S. fit in? If you said it belongs in the low-context communication culture category, then you were right. However, countries can be high-context in one area and low-context in another. Canada, Australia, and most European countries are labeled as low- context. Asian countries like China and Japan, Latin American countries, and many African countries generally fall in the high-context category.

Competent communicators increase their shared environment with the world by learning about other cultures through reading about and communicating with people from various cultures. As mentioned in the Perception chapter, they also remember to decategorize and treat everyone as an individual.

Knowing cultural norms and differences should aid intercultural communication competence. For example, knowing that your Japanese classmates mean no harm when they won't directly answer if they want to go to lunch, will only increase the chances of competent communication. Imagine not knowing that and walking away thinking they were being rude because they won't specifically answer the question.

Key Reflections

After completing the Intercultural classroom exercise, think about how you will use the information you learned about different cultures to communicate more competently with those of different cultures.

Knowledge is power. Knowledge can be gained by listening. The ability to be silent goes hand in hand with active listening. Although one is not inherently better than the other, their comfort with silence gives high-context communicators an advantage when communicating with low context communicators. Competent communicators are able to use low and high-context communication, depending on the situation to achieve positive outcomes.

The study of intercultural communication is becoming more and more important in the U.S. due to the mobility, the growing diversity of organizations and society and developments in technology over time. The growth in interaction of different cultures has led to an increase in interracial marriages, leading us to study marriages/partnerships, the focus of our next and final chapter.

Chapter Activity 11

Intercultural Communication Exercise

Write the Name of the Person Representing Your Host Country and the Names of All Your Group Members:
*If you represented a country, write the names of the individuals from your first group.

-                  -

-                  -

-                  -

-                  -

-                  -

Write Your Individual Question: If you represented, write the country you represented below.

_____

What are the main languages spoken?

_____

Is there any significance to naming or are their naming ceremonies?

_____

Is language (words) valued more than nonverbal/indirect comm. (or silence)?

_____

What are the main religions?

_____

Would you define it as a High Context or Low Context culture?

_____

Write Each Member of Your Group's Individual Question: If you represented, skip this portion.

_____

_____

_____

_____

12

Marriage & Partnership

Population Theory
Soulmates
Different types of Marriages & Partnerships

What You Should Know

What is the World population?

What is the population of California?

Does Population play a role in one's ability to find a mate(s)? Why or why not?

What You Should Do

Activities

- Sign up for a Marriage and Partnership topic.
- Begin researching topic and find at least 5 sources.
- Begin Works Cited page.
- Begin practicing your 3 to 5 minute speeches.

Reflection of the Week
How does the knowledge of "Population theory" effect your outlook on Soulmates?

Introduction

Many people talk about finding their soulmate in life, often referring to the one person that is perfect for them. They are looking to find that one mate that was meant to be with them for the rest of their lives. What is rarely considered are some simple facts that may affect people's ability to find that soulmate they so truly believe exists. Consider the current World and United States populations. According to Census.gov,[1] as of February 2016:

> The world population is over 7.3 Billion while the U.S. population is nearly 323 million. There are about 190 million males and females. If we look at the subsection of people between 18 and 64 years old, that's about 73% of the population or about 262 million people, approximately 131 million males and 131 million females. As of July 2014, there were 39 million people in the state of California alone, with a 50% breakdown of male and female.[2]

Population Theory

This information should suggest just how difficult it might be to find that one soulmate. These numbers can be so intimidating that when considering odds like this, believers often result to having some type of "faith". People may say that a higher power will bring their soulmate to them… somehow… some way.

The other problem plaguing marriages and partnerships today is a lack of communication. Couples tend not to create a shared understanding of what they want the relationship to be, specifically the roles each partner should play. Using written surveys in Interpersonal Communication college courses over many years revealed: people have distinct and varied views on marriage and love. For example, the wide variance of students' answers when asked: what marriage means to them, the specific roles mates should play, to describe love, and the reasons why they believe (or don't believe) in soulmates revealed just how difficult it is to find people that see eye to eye on these topics. For that matter, even finding two people that were flexible in their beliefs was difficult. Even if or when you are lucky enough to find someone with shared beliefs, would the physically attraction to that person be there? Physical attraction can grow over time, but who doesn't enjoy the instant attraction felt when seeing or meeting someone for the first time? Do most people take the time to get to know the person and hope physical attraction comes later? Probably not.

The purpose of this discussion is not to dissuade anyone from the possibility of finding a soulmate or marriage. The goal is to encourage people simply by recognizing the population of the World, the U.S., and their state. If someone believes in soulmates (or is searching for a mate in general), the options of finding a lasting relationship seem to be only limited by your location and level of communication competence.

There are 39 million people in the state of California. About 51% identify as female and 49% identify as male. Consider New York City where there are over 4.2 million possible mates of the opposite or same sex. The sheer numbers make the possibility of finding a soulmate daunting.

111

Consider traveling the world, exposing yourself to the approximate 3.7 billion females and 3.6 billion males? The only thing between you and successfully finding a mate may be taking an Intercultural Communication course or perhaps the high costs of world travel. The point here is that our world is often much larger than we consider it. Our only limits are those that we place on ourselves.

Key Reflections

After reading the chapter and considering the concept of "Population theory", does it affirm or disaffirm your outlook on Soulmates? Why?

Learning about the other communicator and communicating effectively are keys in creating productive relationships. The rest of this lesson is about increasing your shared environment by researching topics related to marriage and partnership.

Chapter Activity 12

Marriages/Partnerships Practices

(Worldwide)

Research Assignment/ Presentation: Due _____

Give a 3 to 5 minute presentation summarizing the information you find most important/interesting from your sources. You must use at least two books (or scholarly journals) as sources plus 3 other sources (not Wikipedia.org or an unapproved .com), and turn in an MLA formatted Works Cited page. Your speech must be delivered extemporaneously using index cards.

Find books, articles, & resources that describe/ analyze your topic choice:
Note: Previous students have found the 5 proper sources necessary for all the topics below

1.   Adulterous Marriages
2.   Arranged Marriage- China
3.   Arranged Marriage- India
4.   Arranged Marriage- Nigeria
5.   Common Law Marriage- State regulations
6.   Commuter Marriages
7.   Divorce Rates- U.S.
8.   Domestic Partnerships- History
9.   Domestic Violence and Marriage- U.S.
10.   Domestic Violence and Marriage- Islamic Cultures
11.   Domestic Violence and Marriage- Latino Community
12.   Forced Marriage- Asian Communities
13.   Forced Marriage- Ethiopia
14.   Forced Marriage- India
15.   Forced Marriage – Pakistan
16.   Interfaith Marriages
17.   Interfamily Marriage/ Inbreeding- U.S. History
18.   Interfamily Marriage/Inbreeding- World History
19.   Interracial Marriage- White & Japanese
20.   Interracial Marriage- U.S. History and today
21.   History of Marriage- Biblical
22.   History of Marriage- Buddhist
23.   History of Marriage- Hebrew
24.   History of Marriage- Hindu
25.   History of Marriage- Historic
26.   History of Marriage- Islamic
27.   Love and Marriage- *When did the concept of Love become considered as a factor in Marriage?*
28.   Mail Order Brides- China
29.   Mail Order Brides- Philippines
30.   Mail Order Brides- Russia
31.   Mail Order Brides- Vietnam
32.   Marriage and U.S. Citizenship
33.   Marriage Ceremonies- Afghanistan
34.   Marriage Ceremonies- El Salvador
35.   Marriage Ceremonies- China
36.   Marriage Ceremonies- Nigeria
37.   Marriage Ceremonies- Philippines
38.   Online Dating- Leading to Marriage
39.   Polyamory
40.   Polyandry- Africa
41.   Polyandry- Malaysia
42.   Polyandry- Tibet
43.   Polygamy- Mali
44.   Polygamy- U.S.
45.   Prenuptial Agreements- History
46.   Prenuptial Agreements- Today
47.   Same Sex Marriage- History in U.S.
48.   Same Sex Marriage- Europe
49.   Soul Mates – Origin

50.   **Soul Mates- Today**
51.   **Pitch a Marriage and/or Partnership Topic- Requires a student to add topic to the list, then submit 5 "proper" sources to instructor at least one week before presentation due date for approval.**

Endnotes

Chapter 1

[1] S. McCornack (2010). Reflect & Relate: An Introduction to Interpersonal Communication. Boston: Bedford/St. Martin's.

[2] S. Cohen, W.J. Doyle, D. P. Skoner, B.S. Rabin, & J. M. Gwalney (1997). "Social Ties and Susceptibility to the Common Cold." *Journal of the American Medical Association, 277,* 1, 940-1, 944.

[3] J. Lynch (1977). *The Broken Heart: The Medical Consequences of Loneliness* (pp. 239-242). New York: Basic Books; see also A. J. Kposowa (200). "Marital Status and Suicide in the National Longitudinal Morality Study." *Journal of Epidemiology and Community Health, 54, 254-261.*

[4] W. D. Rees and S. G. Lutkins (1967). "Morality of Bereavement." *British Medical Journal, 4,* 13.

[5] Three articles in *The Journal of the American Medical Association* 267 (January 22/29, 1992) discuss the link between psychosocial influences and coronary heart disease: R. B. Case, A. J. Moss, N. Case, M. McDermott, & S. Eberly (1992). "Living Alone after Myocardial Infarction," pp. 515-519; R. B. Williams, J. C. Barefoot, R. M. Califf, T. L. Haney, W. B. Saunders, D. B. Pryon, M. A. Hlatky, I. C. Siegler, & D. B. Mark (1992). "Prognostic Importance of Social and Economic Resources among Medically Treated Patients with Angiographically Documented Coronary Artery Disease," pp.520-524; and R. Ruberman (1992). "Psychosocial Influences on Mortality of Patients with Coronary Heart Disease," pp. 559-560; see also J. T. Cacioppo, J. M. Ernst, M. H. Burleson, M. K. McClintock, W. B. Malarkey, L. C. Hawkley, R. B. Kowalewski, A. Paulsen, J. A. Hobson, K. Hugdahl, D. Spiegel, & G. G. Berntson (200). "Lonely Traits and Concomitant Physiological Processes: The MacArthur Social Neuroscience Studies." *International Journal of Psychophysiology, 35,* 143-154.

[6] Lynch, op. cit.

[7] S. McCornack (2010). Reflect & Relate: An Introduction to Interpersonal Communication (pp. 6-11, 20-23). Boston: Bedford/St. Martin's.

[8] S. Lane (2009). Interpersonal Communication: Competence & Competence (pp. 27-29). Boston: Allyn & Bacon.

Chapter 2

[1] R. Adler and R. Proctor (2007). *Looking Out, Looking In* 12th Edition (pp. 27-33). California: Thompson Learning, Inc.

Chapter 3

[1] R. Adler and R. Proctor (2007). *Looking Out, Looking In* 12th Edition (pp. 61-62). California: Thompson Learning, Inc.

[2] J. DeVito (2009). *The Interpersonal Communication Book* (pp. 71-75). Boston, MA: Pearson/Allyn and Bacon.

Chapter 4

[1] S. McCornack (2010). Reflect & Relate: An Introduction to Interpersonal Communication (pp. 78-81). Boston: Bedford/St. Martin's.

[2] R. Adler and R. Proctor (2007). *Looking Out, Looking In* 12th Edition (p. 106). California: Thompson Learning, Inc.

Chapter 5

[1] A. Jensen and S. Trenholm (2004). *Interpersonal Communication* (pp. 88-99). New York: Oxford University Press.

[2] R. Adler and R. Proctor (2007). *Looking Out, Looking In* 12th Edition (pp. 161- 162, 175-177). California: Thompson Learning, Inc.

Chapter 6

[1] Researched summarized by J. K. Burgoon (1994). "Nonverbal Signals." In M. L. Knapp & G. R. Miller (Eds.), Handbook of Interpersonal Communication (p. 235). Newbury Park, CA: Sage.

[2] R. Adler and R. Proctor (2007). *Looking Out, Looking In* 12th Edition (pp. 197-205). California: Thompson Learning, Inc.

[3] K. Floyd (2009). Interpersonal Communication: The Whole Story (pp. 218- 233). Boston: McGraw-Hill.

[4] C. R. Kleinke (1977). "Compliance to Requests Made by Gazing and Touching Experimenters in Field Settings.," Journal of Experimental Social Psychology, 13, 218-223.

Chapter 7

[1] S. McCornack (2010). Reflect & Relate: An Introduction to Interpersonal Communication (pp. 60-67). Boston: Bedford/St. Martin's.

Chapter 8

[1] L. Barker, R. Edwards, C. Gaines, K. Gladney, & R. Holley (1981). "An Investigation of Proportional Time Spent in Various Communication Activities by College Students." Journal of Applied Communication Research, 8, 101-109.

[2] S. Beebe and S. Beebe (2011). Interpersonal Communication: Relating to Others (pp. 197-205). Boston: Allyn & Bacon.

[3] R. Adler and R. Proctor (2007). Looking Out, Looking In 12th Edition (pp. 236-239). California: Thompson Learning, Inc. 4

[4] A. Wovin & C. G. Coakley (1988). Listening, 3rd. ed. (p. 208). Dubuque, IA: W. C. Brown.

Chapter 9

[1] R. Adler and R. Proctor (2007). Looking Out, Looking In 12th Edition (pp. 366-368). California: Thompson Learning, Inc.

[2] J. DeVito (2009). The Interpersonal Communication Book (pp. 278-281). Boston, MA: Pearson/Allyn and Bacon.

[3] R. Adler and R. Proctor (2007). Looking Out, Looking In 12th Edition (pp. 387-391). California: Thompson Learning, Inc.

Chapter 10

[1] R. Adler and R. Proctor (2007). Looking Out, Looking In 12th Edition (pp. 330-331). California: Thompson Learning, Inc.

[2] J. Gottman (2006). "Why Marriages Fail." In K. M. Galvin & P. J. Cooper (Eds.), Making Connections: Readings in Relational Communication, 4th ed. (pp. 228-236). Los Angeles: Roxbury.

[3] R. Adler and R. Proctor (2007). Looking Out, Looking In 12th Edition (pp. 331-340). California: Thompson Learning, Inc.

Chapter 11

[1] E. Hall. Beyond Culture. New York: Doubleday, 1959.

Chapter 12

[1] "U.S. and World Population Clock Tell Us What You Think." Population Clock. United States Census Bureau, n.d. Web. 01 Aug. 2016. http://www.census.gov/popclock/

[2] U.S. Census Bureau, n.d. Web. http://www.census.gov/quickfacts/table/PST045215/06#

Appendix

Interpersonal Communication
Skills Video Screening List

As an important part of this course, we will occasionally have discussion board forums about particular films and television shows. It is your responsibility to see all the videos and answer the significant questions that accompany them. You will not be able to earn all the possible points if you do not. Here is a list of the programs and the time codes you should view to answer the questions:

Film	Time Code
Cast Away (2000):	1:06:45 – 1:15:17
	1:26:35 – 1:31:30
	1:40:33 – 1:45:18
	Total= 19 minutes
Catch Me If You Can (2002):	3:05 – 8:50
	13:06 – 22:46
	31:40 – 40:30
	49:00 – 56:50
	1:52:18 – 1:57:50
	Total= 35 minutes
As Good As It Gets (1997):	0 – 10:07
	10:07 – 14:35
	23:24 – 35:31
	58:28 – 1:02:28
	1:02:28 – 1:07:21
	Total= 35 minutes
Hitch (2005)	0 – 6:42
	14:54 – 19:19
	25:50 – 30:05
	1:23:34 – 1:28:00
	Total= 21minutes
Full Disclosure (2006)	Total = 17:57 minutes
	Starring: Judy Green & Brent Sexton
	Writer/Director: Douglas Horn
	Previously on iTunes (partially on YouTube as "My First Date")

TV Show	Season / Episode
The Office	2 / Conflict Resolution
The King of Queens	8 / Vocal Discord

There are multiple ways to attempt to see these shows; including iTunes or Netflix, if you don't have either (or can't find them there), try On Demand. If you don't have On Demand (or can't find them there), try Hulu, or some other Internet Service. You can also purchase (or in some cases rent) these films/television shows from Amazon.

Works Cited (Example)

(Your Name) Prof. Thompson Comm 20 (Date)

Works Cited (Presentation Topic)

"Blueprint Lays Out Clear Path for Climate Action." *Environmental Defense Fund*.
    Environmental Defense Fund, 8 May 2007. Web. 24 May 2009.

Celello, Kristin. *Making Marriage Work: A History of Marriage And Divorce In The*
    Twentieth- Century United States. Chapel Hill: The University of North Carolina Press,
    2009. *eBook Collection (EBSCOhost)*. Web. 18 Nov. 2015.

GAUVREAU, DANIELLE, and PATRICIA THORNTON. "Marrying 'The Other': Trends And
    Determinants of Culturally Mixed Marriages In Québec, 1880-1940." *Canadian Ethnic*
    Studies 47.3 (2015): 111-141. *Academic Search Premier*. Web. 18 Nov. 2015.

"marriage." *Encyclopedia Britannica. Britannica Academic*. Encyclopedia Britannica Inc., 2015.
    Web. 18 Nov. 2015.
    <http://0academic.eb.com.webpac.peralta.edu/EBchecked/topic/366152/marriage>.

Uzawa, Hirofumi. *Economic Theory and Global Warming*. Cambridge: Cambridge UP, 2003.
    Print.

4 Methods to Deliver a Great Speech

www.definiscommunications.com

When it comes to delivering your presentation, you actually have many choices. Public speaking involves so much more than just standing in front of a crowd and talking. How you deliver your thoughts and message can depend on a number of factors, such as your comfort level, the nature of the information and most important, your audience's expectations. So before you stand up to speak, make sure you choose the correct delivery method that will give you the best results for you and your audience.

Here is a quick overview of each method:

Reading verbatim from a manuscript

Some speeches must be delivered word for word, such as critical updates to the media, reports at a professional meeting or a political address. In these highly formal situations accuracy is extremely important because every word will be analyzed by the press, the public and the audience. Good speech writers know the importance of writing speeches that will be read and how to create them.

It may look easy to give this kind of speech, but it requires a great deal of skill. The trick is to make the written word sound spontaneous—to make the words come alive. Otherwise, this type of speech and the words can come across as dry and dispassionate, and the speaker can ap- pear stiff and uncomfortable. If you are going to read a speech, careful rehearsal is mandatory. The delivery must be closely choreographed with the message to lift the speech from the page and into the hearts and minds of the listeners.

Memorization

Hundreds of years ago, the legendary orators would memorize long and complex speeches and deliver them word for word. Fortunately, today this is not a customary or recommended practice. For short speeches like introductions of other speakers, wedding toasts, thank you comments or congratulatory remarks it's okay to memorize and sometimes helpful to do so. And there may be certain sections of a longer talk that you may want to memorize, like the opening, the closing and the transitions. If you do recite any part of your speech from memory make sure that you know it cold so you don't run the risk of fumbling, getting off track and losing your connection to your audience.

Impromptu

An impromptu speech is delivered without any preparation at all. Most people would rather not do an impromptu speech, but they often cannot be avoided. In business meetings your ideas and opinions might be solicited on the spot. But rest assured that we all give hundreds of impromptu speeches every day. This "on the spot" speech is the core of everyday conversation. So if someone turns to you and asks for your thoughts, don't panic. Take a deep breath and think through a logical beginning, middle and ending progression. Keep the audience on track by stressing key words: "The first point I'd like to cover…" "Next you will see…" "And finally I would like to add…" Impromptu speaking takes practice, but if you follow a structure you'll soon get the hang of it.

Extemporaneous

While many people think extemporaneous and impromptu are the same since they are both speeches that are not read or memorized, there is one key difference. The impromptu speech is completely off the cuff; the extemporaneous speech is thoughtfully prepared, planned and practiced.

When speaking extemporaneously, the speaker uses notes, an outline or a PowerPoint slide presentation to stay on track. And as long as your speech structure is carefully planned, that's all you need. This is the method we recommend for the majority of people we work with. Once   you have the content prepared you can spend your time practicing the flow of the material and your delivery. As you practice out loud, the words will come out differently with each run through but you will know the basic sentence structure and logical progression of the material. If you practice enough, the most effective parts of your message will stick in your mind and come out as you planned. The key here is to take the time to fully prepare. No short cuts! When you practice, you will have full control of your topic, sound convincing and yet still come across with a spontaneous and conversational tone.

Ultimately, the speech delivery method you choose will depend on many factors, such as how formal or informal the presentation is, how well you know your subject, who the audience is, and your own comfort level. When you take the time to analyze these factors and educate yourself about your choices, you can make the best decision about what method to use and give a great speech.